the Time Capsule

The Strides of Man

Norman W. Smith
Illustrated by Ivan Hinds

Copyright © 2024 **Norman W. Smith Publishing**

All rights reserved. No part of this publication may be reproduced, distributed, or transmitted in any form or by any means, including photocopying, recording, or other electronic or mechanical methods, without the prior written permission of the publisher, except in the case of brief quotations embodied in critical reviews and certain other noncommercial uses permitted by copyright law. For permission requests, write to the publisher, addressed "Attention: Book Rights and Permission," at the address below.

Published in the United States of America

ISBN 978-1-962569-61-3 (SC)
ISBN 978-1-962569-59-0 (HC)
ISBN 978-1-962569-60-6 (Ebook)

Norman W. Smith Publishing
355 East 194th St
Apt 6E Bronx NY 10458
nwsjamaica@aol.com

Ordering Information and Rights Permission:

Quantity sales. Special discounts might be available on quantity purchases by corporations, associations, and others. For details, contact the publisher at the address above.

For Book Rights Adaptation and other Rights Permission. Call us at 6463844616 or send us an email at nwsjamaica@aol.com

I dedicate this book to my wonderful
Children

To my son, Kashife, whose fortitude and willingness to try has inspired me. Your honesty is astounding, for never in your life have I ever found you in the position where you found it necessary to compromise your integrity. To me, that means much more than my feeble words can ever express. Neither can I, with any degree of sincerity, remember having that experience before. I love you dearly.

~

To my daughter, Yanese, with ambition as high as the sky and a sense of independence that matches. Those, and the other qualities you possess, I admire greatly. With the hope that I may one day acquire some of your characteristics, for they are indeed admirable, and I love you dearly.

~

To Travis, your meekness is an uncommon quality, and your love for music makes me think of you as King David with his harp, and I hope you will inherit the world of goodness. Allow no one to persuade you from the qualities you possess. Those unique qualities make you who you are. I love you dearly.

Contents

Preface	viii
The Time Capsule	1
The Strides of Man	3
Mother	4
The Question	6
The Lighthouse	7
Traveling	10
A Dreary Day	12
A Gift	13
Cherry Hill	14
Sell me a Dream	15
The Vulture	19
A Cursed Womb	21
The Rainbow	23
A Lonely Craft	24
A Man's Castle	25
A New Nation	26
Then Now and After	28
Africa	31
Plantation Seduction	32
Blood, Sweat, and Tears	33
A New York Summer	34
Indoor Garden	37
Passing of Time	38
Sleep Forever	39
Words and Principles	40
Ventilating with My Pen	41
USMC Brothers	42
A Warrior's Prayer	45
A Seed of Hope	46
My Dreamworld	47
A Natural High	49
Again	51
Aged	52
Ahead	53
Among Us	54

Angels	55
As Romans Do	56
A Sailor's Plight	59
Atlantic	60
My Children	62
My Late Pen	64
Listen to New York	66
Keeper of the City	68
Christmas for Two by the Fire	69
Stolen by the Master	70
Master Rooster	74
Starting Over	76
The Spices of Life	78
The Earth	79
Awful Nights	80
Barack Obama	81
Wounded Wings	83
The Gallows	84
Warriors' Mothers	88
DWI Victims	90
Polly and the Bee	92
Fred	93
Hunting the Hunter	94
Lost Valentine	96
Natural Beauty	98
The Shepherd's Light	99
Markings of Time	102
The Indian's Plight	103
The Eskimo Hunter	104
The Casted Lot	106
Village Child	108
Life	109
After All	111
An Empty Chair	112
Ancient Man	113
Waves	115
April	116
As We Behold	117
At First	118
At Midnight	119

At Peace	120
Beauty	121
Black and White	122
Blue Caribbean	124
Booth Hill	126
Boredom	127
Broken Limb	128
Broken Spell	129
Bubbles	130
Building a Village	131
Cease-Fire	133
The Night's Farewell	136
My Ancestors' Spirit	138
Three Days	140
Each Day	141
Metaphorical Mountain	143
Redemption	144
The house Prisoner	145
The Hermit	146
The Frog and the Crocodile	147
Compass Plan	148
The Phoenix	149
This Moment	153
The Nightingales	154
Houses of Dreams	155
Crippled	156
Cry	158
Intrusion	159
Paradise	160
Seduction by a Queen	161
Retrospect	165
Open Doors	166
Overcast	168
Striving	170
Fire Men	171
First Kill	172
Half-Open	174
Halves	175
In the Shadow	176
Infinite Now	178

Innocence Lost	181
Jack Frost	182
Just Before Sunset	183
Know Myself	184
Mango Season	185
My Pride	186
Ransom	187
Snow White	188
Sweet Chariot	189
The Forest Dweller	191
The Little Flame	192
The Little Voice	195
The Clown	196
Seven Days	197
Show Your Love	198
Sir Gallant	200
Sleep	202
The Street Corner	203
The Statue	204
The Stallion	207
The Shepherd's Light	208
The Rose	209
The Red Oak Tree	210
About the Author	212

Preface

With all that the universe has to offer, there is no telling how much longer its generosity will hold out. From one generation to another, the wondrous resilience of this seemingly indestructible earth is diminishing. The evidence is all around us and even more prevalent in mankind's behavior toward the growing changes of the planet Earth.

It is very compelling when one's approach is not to save the world but to share the way countries, societies, communities, neighborhoods, families, and individuals existed before the destruction of this universe. There is no guarantee that there will be a survivor to tell of what the world was like. So, it's here, *The Time Capsule*.

A volume of life-spelling words that could offer a guide for rebuilding. A special collection, rich with the operations and functions of existence, of life and time. Lifetime. *The Time Capsule* spanning generations and touching on evolution. Showing the brilliance and resourceful nature of both man and the universe.

The Time Capsule will stimulate one's imagination and could encourage investigation at various scholastic levels. *The Time Capsule*.

A special thanks to Eva Hinds, who dedicated her time and continued to give endless encouragement to the preparation and distribution of this book.

The Time Capsule

Exposed to the finer things of life

Developed a passion for botany

That consumed most of his time

In his cellar, he grows a garden
With orchids and exotic plants.

There in command of his pen

As the next passion of his life

The one he holds as his dearest

Frequently he spends an entire day
Writes from morning until night.

Never left his beloved sanctuary

Of his garden and his favored pen

One day at noon, he heard a blast
He peeped through the window
Only to notice that it was dark.

Perhaps the blast of a thunderstorm

Like the others this, too, will pass

Engulfed by his writing he heeded not
But continued until the morning
Again, he peeped through his window.

It seemed to have grown much darker

With that, he laid aside his pen

To ponder what it might have been

Yes, the fear had reached him now

Perplexed, he scratched his weary head.

Once again but now in fear he peeped

Through the dampened cellar window
To notice the absent of life outside

When many days had passed and gone
He went upstairs and exited his home.

There, the first to greet his eyes

A book he wrote, the time capsule

Speechless, he stood alone and scared

Embarking upon the only obvious quest
To see what has become of man.

The Strides of Man

From the paradise of Eden's garden,
First introduced to this our world
To the land of Sodom,
Where we were almost extinct,
Our journey thus far
I have embraced as the strides of man.
If we were Introduced by creation,
We have risen and fallen.

And if by evolution,
From our four
Planted on the ground,
To now our upward stand.
Our journey thus far
Is still gigantic in the strides of man,
From apes to modern man,
From caves to the towers we climbed,
Evolving from mumbling mute
To fluent and eloquent tongue.

Creation or evolution,
The Big Bang or Eden's garden paradise,
Planting our footprints on the moon,
To splitting of the atom;
A journey we all should be proud of,
Known as the strides of man.
But we have tainted our hands
Spilling the blood of our fellowman.
As Cain slew his brother Abel
And spilled blood upon the virgin land
To the mountain of Afghanistan,
Where a war we now pursue
With bombs and automatic rifles,
We are on our downward slope,
Fast approaching the extinction of man.

Mother

It's not too long ago since I realized
How much she meant to me,
But it's been a long time since I have noticed
The gentleness and kindness she had shown to me.

The load she carried must have been heavy and fatiguing. Only a mother could have known,
And though being loved by my daddy,
He couldn't have helped her share that load.

The load upon her head must have been heavy too
With nine months of wondering, "Will God see me through?" Yet she bore the anguish and pain and brought me to this world And showed me her love far beyond compare.

Looking back at my childhood,
I can't but remember how sweet it used to be
When she clutched me with her warm and tender arms
And lay me on her breasts to rest.

When her nipples were my only source of living,
She fed me day and night
Without letting me out of her sight.
Oh, what fortitude she had.

And oftentimes when I was sad, she sang to me
Little songs that always made my heart glad.
How could I forget her? No reason could ever be.
I love the ways she taught me
And adore the day she brought me.

The Question

What if? Ask yourself or someone else.
This question presents quite a challenge.
What then? Should one just falter and let it be?
Or ponder upon it with careful thoughts?
What if you have failed in your thinking.

    And unable to resolve those two simple words?
    And too many sunrises and sunsets have passed with
    What if? Still trapped in your mind?
    What if the question was never asked?
    What if the challenge you did not ponder upon?

These two simple words remains a mystery.
What if world without end is meant to be
A world without dimension, that of infinite size?
Or what if world without end was meant to be
A world where there is no end to time but eternity?
Would it be large enough to accommodate us
As we continue to multiply.

    What if the aging process should discontinue,
    With everyone remaining as they are?
    Would it be fair to the infant
    Who would never be able to grow up
    And experience the different stages of life?

What if our imagination could transform into reality?
Just think of it and it is done.
What if there were no death and life continued forever?
What if there were no wars, and all was peace and serene?
What if the Creator, with his infinite wisdom,
Had created evolution in his master plan
After he had made man?

The Lighthouse

Perched upon the peak
Of some dismal rocky shore
Often secluded there you will find,
Proudly standing
And vigilantly giving a watchful eye
Overlooking the sea,
A lighthouse—the watchdog of the sea.

Decorated in white for all the world to see,
Shining its majestic beam from shore to sea
In hopes of aiding
Some bewildered ship to see
A navigable path
Safely to the port they seek.

Helping to avoid the perils that lurk
Beyond and beneath the fearful waves,
I am a beacon—my quest is
Some troubled soul to save.
May my gleaming light a pilot be,
For ships which without my light
Would be doomed at sea.
With glittering rays
From wave to wave,

Flashing streams of light
That seem to touch the horizon.
From a distance, my tower appears
To be touching the sky.
I am a beacon—my quest is
Some troubled soul to save,
No distinction have I made between friend and foe.

I have hosted them all—with open arms
I have welcomed many strangers to my shore,
Sheltered them in my humble abode;
But if by chance you heed not my warning,
Or if my light you do not see;
If you should fall victim to this dismal shore
And run aground or smash upon
A treacherous rock,
Then in earnest may God your pilot be
And guard you to safety.

Traveling

Traveling, traveling, I am still traveling on.
With grim determination I must travel on
Along this road of life, where most of the journey
Is a challenging hill
With its many perilous precipices,
landslides, quicksand, and mire.
I must take heed and plant my feet firmly
Where they will not slip,
Lest I stumble and plunge to my death.

I have met others on the way
Who fell victim, lost their courage
And laid down and perished
Because their predecessors
Left no tracks, no maps,
Or landmarks for the journey
Upon which they embarked.
In that they lost their will to fight,
They relinquished their hold on life
And surrendered to death.

But I refuse to grant death so vague a victory.
No, not as long as I am able
To breathe a single breath of air.
I shall not cease until a victory I have won.
Traveling, traveling, I must continue to travel on
Visions of hope I now can see.
Indeed, frequently they visit me
Dreams of victory now dwell
Where doubt and despair once resided.

Faith and patience I have adopted
For my companions and constant guides while I stride.
Hand in hand we travel, side by side.
As my strength decreases, my courage increases.
When my weary feet falter and I stumble,
I summon all my will
To help me climb life's challenging hill.

Oftentimes I wonder
If there is an end to life's journey,
Or just a new beginning of a different phase
To a higher plane,
And when all hope seems gone and burdened with gloom
In the midst of all despair, there shines a gleam of hope.

The sun begins to rise, peeping through the clouds,
Shining its rays around. A welcoming sight to see.
I gaze and gaze upon it,
Transfixed with awe for some minutes,
Suspended in time as if
Time had stopped for a moment,
When a gentle voice whispers to me and says,
"Lo, I am with you always."

All along my journey my Savior was with me,
And now a mountain to me
Is just a valley, turned upside down.
Far off in the distance, is that Mount Kilimanjaro?
Or could it be the peak of Mount Everest I see?
It really matters not to me,
My guide and Savior travels with me.

A Dreary Day

Such a dreary day,
On a cold and wintery December
The sun stays in, it refuses to shine.
Only its silhouette you can see,
But not its rays on this wintery December,
A dense blanket of cloud
Offered itself, a shadow gloom.

The wind lays still and silent.
Not a moving patch of cloud,
No fluttering of the leaves.
The trees stand without a sway,
No birds in the sky to hunt or play
On this cold dreary day.

The rain is falling constantly
But never reaches the earth.
It dissipates among the dreary dense clouds,
Thus forming a fog.
While down below us poor creatures feel
We have been robbed, of our golden sunlight glow
On this dreary wintery day.

A Gift

Look at what we have been given!
   A little speck of love from heaven,
      Sent to us that we should nurture.
         And that speck, with the proper care,
            May someday turn into a flame.
               A bonfire, or perhaps a wildfire.

Whatever flame it may turn out to be,
   We must remember to handle it with care.
      That speck of love, with the proper care,
         May someday turn into a glowing star,
            Or perhaps a galaxy, or even the Milky Way.

And so we nurture our speck of love
   With gentleness, for each other we care.
      Thus we toil, and with our hands
         We built ourselves a cottage.
         And there we watch
            Our love as it grows.

Soon we produce children of love,
   And now with love we often pray.
      While we give thanks to the heavens
         For that little speck it has given.
            Now a family of love we share.

Cherry Hill

Cherry Hill on high, exhibiting her splendor,
Boasting her charming view, dazzling the eyes
At sunrise or at sunset.

You will behold her at her best,
And during the course of the day
Her extraordinary beauty she displays.

Beauty that upstages the neighboring view.
Cherry Hill on high, where many are conceived
And lots of fair maidens have been deceived.

While cherries are being reaped
Upon this forever charming hill
Twinkling stars, with their lights gleaming.

Roaring cars, with their headlights beaming,
Some hiding under the shadow of the night,
Playing lovers songs, and wishing upon
Each shooting star they see.

That their union will last forever.
Some soon to regret the fruit they yield,
Some conceiving while being deceived.

Wishing they could reclaim the fruit
They allowed to be picked on Cherry Hill,
And cursed the hill for their visit
And the virtue they have lost.

Sell me a Dream

Mr. Dream Merchant, please sell me a dream
And please make it an expensive one.
Cheapness is not for me.
Please tailor it especially for me,
No one else should it fit.
Make it all cash, credit doesn't seem to work.

Maybe if I invest someone else's hard-earned dollar,
It may come true at last.
Cash and carry is the way to go.
Credit has too much interest and delay,
And my credit score is too low anyway.

Let it be lighting quick.
I am running out of time
And I need it like yesterday.
I will put in a few more dollars,
Please send it by express.
My patience is running thin,
And I can't afford to lose this bid.

Mr. Dream Merchant, I have no time to waste or wait,
The anticipation is getting strong.
Please send some painkillers,
I don't want to feel a thing.
And please include some tranquilizers
So I can pass the time with sleep.

I have wasted a lot of years, and nothing have I gained.
I don't want to work too hard
For success, easy does it, I say.
Contrary to popular belief, laziness is my way.
So while you are working on my dream,
It would be grand if you can find
Someone to dream, my dream for me.

Don't want to work too hard for success.
Let me rest on my back relaxing under a shady tree.
Sit me down in a cool meadow,
Or in a cozy air-conditioned room
Where I don't have to sweat
Just enjoy the luxurious lazy way.

*The captain worries not
About the depth of the ocean
While his ship is afloat, but of the length
Of his anchor chain, if it will hold.*

The Vulture

In a class by himself
And as such, it is called unique
No one envies them for their job,
One that is in high demand.
They perch upon the highest tree or cliff
Overlooking their targeted domain.

Usually on the outskirts of town,
And frequently circling the perimeters
In high hopes of discovering a meal.
Wishing for death to call some creature
So that they can eat and be merry,
Always finding a station upwind
Since the wind is their most reliable messenger
To their keen sense of smell.

Though most people favored other birds
For their splendid colors
Such as the peacock and the cockatoo,
And for food, they favored the chicken
Turkey, ducks, quails, and the pheasant.
And the other exotic birds, they choose as pets,
We are glad they resent us.

So our species can gamely flourish
While we enjoy our freedom.
No hunting for game and ending up
On a platter, or cooped up on a farm,
Or perhaps stuffed and mounted on a wall,
Or caged, in some lonesome house.
But we are as free as birds should be.
Unlike those edible birds they favored,
Neither two legs, four legs, man or beast,
Welcome us at their table for feast,
Or as their caged pet to keep.

Though we possess no great talent in flight
No gift of speed, or tenacity to fight,
No acrobatic maneuvers or unusual skills,
We are the most unlikely bird to be killed.

Often the eagle passes us on their way to hunt,
Sometimes returning unsuccessfully
Still not looking in our direction
Quiet as a mouse, on the job each day
Eating to keep your city clean is our pay.
We pose no threat to any living thing,
Harmless as a dove they say.

They even forget about the importance of our job
And that's all right,
Thanks to man, their law protects us
Thou shall not kill the vulture, so they say.
And that's the law in all the land,
I do believe that men are smart
Who will do my job if I become extinct.

A Cursed Womb

A white house and picket fence
Serves as a landmark in an affluent neighborhood.
No loitering on the streets
And no police walking the beat.

With flamingos, swans, and exotic fish
Parading in their pond
While peacocks stroll their manicured lawn,
With no children to play hide-and-seek
Among the well-pruned trees.

The bittersweet love their hearts can feel,
When with pleasure their eyes behold,
Children playing in glee.
Content and jolly, no fears or cares.

May angels their guardian be,
While their grieving hearts in constant plea
To open the portal of a cursed womb.
Two souls that needs to be a family
In a house they hope to be a home.

If only her womb could be blest
And bear them fruits of their own.
No giggling, shouting, screaming, or laughter.
No jeering, cheering, yelling, or applauding.

The voices of children are absent from the ears.
No sharing of joy on the well-manicured lawn
And the lonely golden retriever stand silent and still
With no children with which to play.
The cursed womb had reaped a spell
When first a fetus life the parents expelled
And locked the portal, no ins or out

And now an infertile womb, a deserted tomb.

Fancy cars in their driveway parked.
They fashioned rubies, diamonds, and cultured pearls.
Many precious jewels upon them are bestowed,
But a cursed barren womb never to be restored.

The Rainbow

That colorful arc displays itself in the sky,
One of nature's most exciting creations
That stimulates our curiosity
And leads us to awesome wondering
Just how Mother Nature paints this way.

With her seven primary colors in the sky
Arching over the oceans, lakes, and seas?
Vivid colors as bright as the stars in the sky,
One day it's there, and the next it's gone.
Where did that colorful arch go,
And why did it leave us so soon?
Its presence has graced us for less than a day.
Then without a warning, it is gone.

Did it disappear, or did it move to somewhere?
No marks remain, not even a single blot,
That beautiful and yet illusive work of art
Nature paints on its canvas, the sky.

Those rainbows often come in a full circle.
But seldom, if ever, have they revealed their all
And grant us a treat to our eyes.
The rainbow, an arc painted in the sky.

A Lonely Craft

A lonely craft battling a storm
Trying to find its way home
As it ventured across a channel.
With a single man as its captain, mate, crew, and cargo,
What would prove a difficult task for a crew of four
Now seems an impossible feat for one.

With a single crew and the absence of cargo,
His vessel so light, all throughout the night,
He fought a gallant fight to keep his vessel afloat.
And the lighthouse on the hill in his sight
But as he got weary, his strength failed.
He collapsed and his little craft began to drift.

With the absence of his wit, the lonely craft
Fell to the will of the storm, and indeed
It showed no mercy, but tossed his vessel about
Like a leaf in that rugged white channel.
But when at last the morning came
And the sun shines down on his face,

A single man, as captain, mate, crew, and cargo.
Lay flat on his back, in his little vessel,
Still absent of his mind.
With his Irish hound licking on his face
To welcome him home.
In time he was awakened, by a man's best friend.

A Man's Castle

Away from the hustling and bustling crowd,
He opened the door and entered his castle
And locked the crazy world outside.
Now to concentrate on what is inside.
Because within these walls lies his all
The family that he loves most dearly.

For in his castle he reigns as the king
With his other half, the castle's queen.
Together they rule in their domain.
Thus side by side they stand,
Not one above and the other below,
Or one in front and the other behind.

If only as his nightly paradise
Within his walls, he enjoys his sanctuary
There in his castle in bliss he stares
At portraits of many revered ancestors
That decorate his castle walls.
And often he would mumble to them.

"Look at who you have made possible."
Then he would point to, or touch
Some of the infants, or later birth
To link the early past, to the tranquil now.
Often, he would take the princes and princesses
And teach them the chain of the generation.

A New Nation

When in search of freedom to worship,
They fled from their British homeland
And landed on this foreign soil called America.

They adopted it as their new home,
The British crown hunted them like hounds
And imposed their taxes, a burden upon them.

But they, like oxen, bore the harness;
And when they could no longer
Suffer so great an imposition.

They refused to pay the taxes demanded,
Denouncing taxation without representation
Is bound to be unfair.

Thus they were viciously attacked
And, like heroes they fought back.
From that they emerged a stronger nation.

Known as the United States of America.
When we were again attacked in Pearl Harbor
We, with vigor, fought back again as heroes.

And from our experience
We have grown even stronger,
And we always will.

Again on 911, when the terrorists
Struck their malicious blow.
Yes, we were badly wounded.

But they never broke our resilient spirit.
For again, from those vicious attacks
We arose a stronger nation.

Bound to survive
Again each time renewing our loyal unity,
And we are still growing stronger.

Then Now and After

As time rolls by like the water
        Springing from a fountain in the earth,
                Or rapidly flowing from a waterfall
                        One way never to return to its source.

And so likewise as living mortals
        We were destined to follow the trend.
                As time rolls by from birth to death
                        We mold our after then from the now.

For the seeds we planted in our then
        Are the fruits we are reaping now,
                While we spring from our fountain birth
                        We are rapidly growing until to the earth we fall.

Be particularly mindful of the deeds we sow,
        For if they are bitter, foul, or sweet,
                In time we will live to reap and eat them.
                        Will they disturb our palates or caress them?

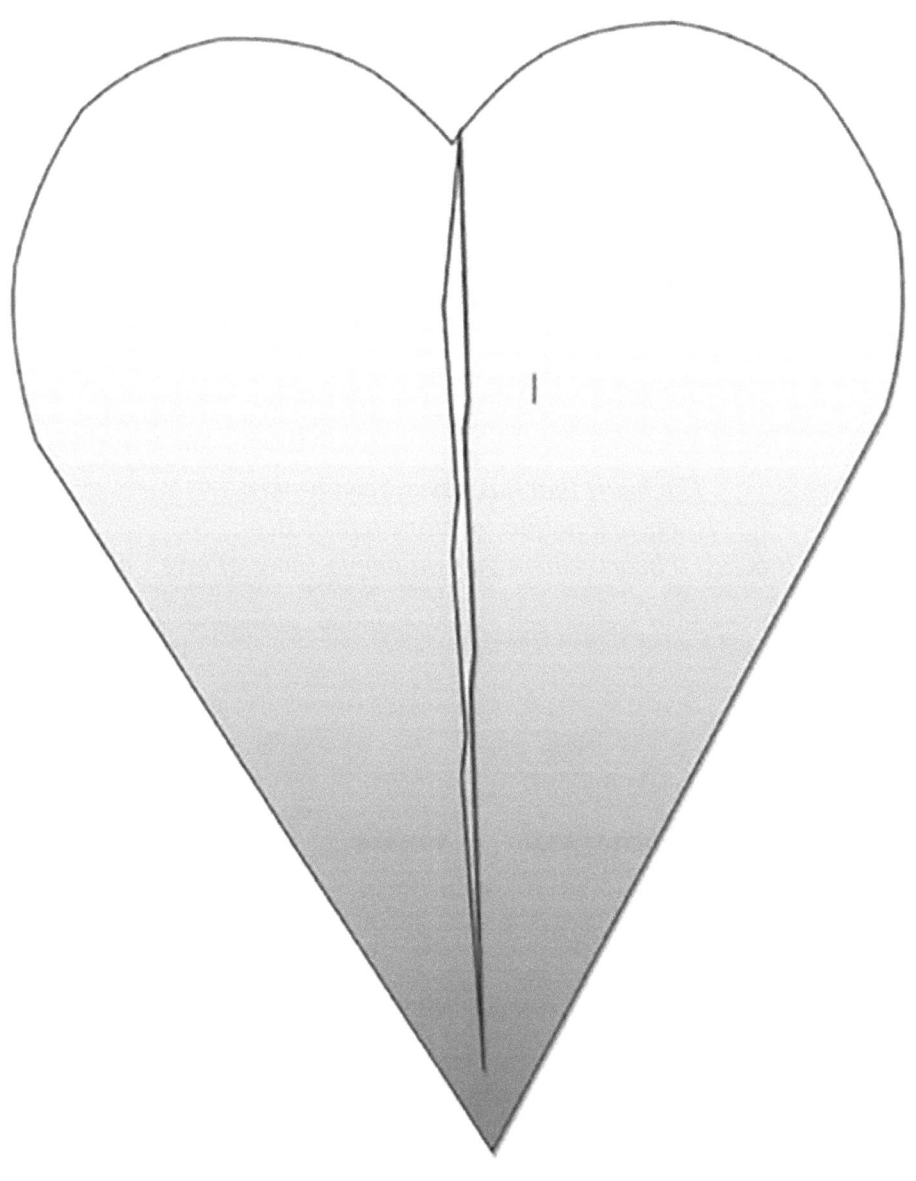

The Time Capsule: The Strides of Man

*The heart that has never been broken
Is a heart, neither of stone nor of steel;
It is just a heart, which gets an ample share of love.*

Africa

Africa, the cradle of civilization!
From its bowels flow the great Niles.
Four thousand one hundred and sixty miles,
Three tributaries combine.

The Blue Nile, the Atbara, and the White Nile.
The father of Africa's rivers,
The vein, through which flows the life
Of several African countries. The Nile!

Africa's pride, spewing its contents
Through its mouth into the Mediterranean.
The valley of kings, along the banks of the Nile,
Noble, Nubian-bred, brave sons.

Africa, exhibiting the largest waterfall in the world.
The great Victoria Falls.
With fame entrusted, not self-imposed
But by visitors proclaiming it to be.

The most beautiful place on earth!
South Africa's Victoria Falls.
Africa: Land of the mighty Mount Kilimanjaro,
With its three volcanoes, wearing its white snowcap.

Blending with the smoke expelled
From its three volcanoes back grounded
By cloudless blue sky, in infinity portrays
Africa, the land of the Sahara untamed,
But not uninhabited nor abandoned.

Plantation Seduction

For the pleasure she seeks
And the possible death he may reap
When upon her mare
Across the field she cantered
Searching for an ebony man
To quench her lustful pleasure
For life or death, the higher the stakes
The more daring a risk she takes.

For when in the fields they lay
On beds fashioned with
Cotton, hay, or dried banana leaves.
If conceived while mere pleasure she seeks,
No stripes upon his back
Can ease the disgrace from the master's head.

And so a rope she plotted for the neck.
To do or to die, to dangle from a tree
Until they are dead.
Dare to say no to the master's wife
Dare to attempt to preserve his life.
To say no would mean
Inviting screams of attempting to take.

And off to that wretched hanging tree
To be hanged anyway, and if she conceived
While her sinful pleasure she pursued,
Without a doubt the master's wrath
Someone will reap.
Infant, mother, or ebony man the slave,
A grave awaiting someone, if not the lot.

Blood, Sweat, and Tears

That by our sweat we shall earn our daily bread
We wept, toiling through our bondage in Egypt
And sin, when Cain first desecrated the earth
With the innocent blood of his brother Abel.

    Thus blood, sweat, and tears,
    Have been with us all the way,
    Constantly throughout the years,
    From Eden's garden where we first began
    When man molded from clay became a living soul.

To the here and now, by his grace we stand,
While neither flight, plight, or fright
Will they cease to exist. Blood sweat and tears,
Committed until death, with us remain
And never before shall we part.

    Though fears often bring with it blood and tears
    And through our body flows a unique identity,
    An historic chart that links us to our ancestors,
    That which is known to us as our DNA
    The architect and constructor of our character.

When our emotions run wild our tears begin to flow
Or if our blood boils hot, and our anger we show
Regardless of the reason, or whatever the season
Blood, sweat, and tears will forever remain
Linked from our past to our future
As well as our DNA fingerprint.

A New York Summer

New York City.
When spring yields its way to the summer,
The Big Apple now begins to bake
With the sweltering heat of the concrete jungle;
Where the hunter and the prey
Intermingled night and day;
In the city that never sleeps.

New York City.
The Liberty City they called it,
When the scorching summer comes around
And the water hydrants are flowing
To cool the concrete jungle;
Where the streets become a paradise
With children swarming the fire hydrants
Like fawns in a desert oasis

New York City.
In the summer, when some of the hydrants
Are sprinkling like lawn sprinklers
While others are rushing, like miniature rapids
To cool the temperature,
Of the sweltering concrete jungle;
Where the public pools are few and far apart
And often so crowded it seems impossible to get in.

New York City.
When passing sports cars,
With their convertible tops down,
Make a turn, or backup to avoid a disaster,
While others roll their windows up
And stop under the waterfall for a quick wash,
Or a chance to cool off, at the manmade temporary oasis.

                New York City.
     When the apartments are like hot ovens
      And the electricity surges off and on;
With barbecue grills on the balconies and sidewalks,
Are a common display, and the children play fight
       With water balloons or water guns;
         Girls skipping double Dutch
And the double-decker buses are crammed with tourists
   And fleets of Circle Liners parade our harbor
         And cruise the Hudson River.

New York City.
In the summer, when the melting pot is at its very best,
And each park represents a village
A mosaic, depicting out of many one?
With the smell of barbecue sauce,
Jerk seasoning, curry, and various herbal composites
Perfuming the air.
With puffs of smoke curl and climb upward
Resembling an Indian or African village of our not-so-distant past;
The aroma of different cultural fragrances
Represents their ethnicity
Tantalizes the nostrils, soon to soothe the palate.

   The Big Apple, New York City, the melting pot of the USA
           As the summer heat intensifies,
           Making its mark on the season,
         The melting pot upstages the world,
            Exhibiting our many cultures;
  A multicolor mosaic showing humanity at its best,
    Parading with music dancing and fashion.
The Saint Patrick's Day parade, the old granddad of them all,
        With its deeply rooted Irish heritage,
           A trademark green and plaid
Along with its unique sound of the bagpipe and fiddle;
 A splendid treat to behold, at summer in New York.

The West Indian parade,
With its peacock-like colorful designs
And chanting dances of their ancestral home;
With the captivating rhythm of the reggae beat,
And its awesome drum and base;
Or the settled steel drum that mimics the piano
Contributing to the splendor of New York summer.

        The upbeat of the hot Latino Salsa dance and music;
          The Dominican and the Puerto Rican parades,
    Their vibrant rainbow of color and fast high-pitched music
       Composed with tweeters, shakers, and Congo drums;
              Their eye-catching fashion
        Combined with other Latinos of New York.
          Their contributions are immense.
         New York summer, a fun place to be.
          In our harbor stands our Queen,
            The goddess of Liberty.

Indoor Garden

The shocked maid
Was astonished to see,
The mistress and her gardener
Watering and pruning
Her interior garden
From the posterior
With pleasure inside the foyer.
Filled with shame,
The mistress proclaimed.

I am afraid, my dear
But you must be fired.
And please be mindful
Never to return to be rehired
Or my husband will learn
Of the jewels you have stolen
While the gardener and I
Were enjoying attending to my garden.

I will be quite generous
And write you a check
Far in excess of your earnings.
So please take my advice
And put a bridle on your tongue,
Never to mention
My garden to anyone.

There are people in high places
Who immensely enjoy
Attending my beautiful,
Delightful garden.
You would be wise
For taking my advice in departing
And pretending never to have seen
My gardener and I, watering my garden.

Passing of Time

Though time goes by quite slowly,
It leaves its mark behind.
And in some cases, it is subliminal,
For I have watched myself growing
And completely having no clue.

It was submerged below
My subconscious mind
And, like good wine, as it aged
With time, it became even better.
I have aged and mellowed with the time.

It is only now in retrospect
That I have seen the leaps and bounds
By which I have recently grown.
It is not modest to be too bold
Or to pat oneself on the back.

I hope there is no such perception.
It was certainly not my intention,
And so with all my sincere earnestness
I thank the powers that be
For the passing of time, though sublime it may be.

Sleep Forever

Sleep your peaceful sleep,
That one they call death.
The same sleep that kisses you
Just before it takes your last breath,
Weaning you from an earthly life,
One of constant labor, fret, and pain.

Sleep that peaceful sleep,
For it is but the portal
Through which we all must exit,
Leading us to a different world
Where we must shed this corruptible
Earthly mortal cloak of flesh.

Sleep thou that peaceful sleep,
Transport us to that different world,
That realm where only immortals dwell.
Where words are often neglected,
And voices are infrequently used.
There they communicate telepathically.

Sleep your peaceful sleep.
From this you shall rise no more
Not as mortals but as immortals,
There to dwell in that heavenly bliss.
So sleep, sleep, sleep, forever sleep
Sleep your last peaceful sleep.

Words and Principles

Should folly fall upon my eyes
And thus deceive my thinking,
Then would cease my words
From being my bond of sincerity
And compromise the principles
Upon which I firmly stand.
Thus, vague would become my pride
Think with my eyes, and not my brain.
To judge with my eyes, and not my heart.
Rejecting that which I feel, to entertain
What may well be an optical illusion.
When my thoughts become my beliefs,
They also become my words,
My bond of sincerity.
Then I can do no more,
Than to live by them.
Often I scribe them on paper
And at times, I utter them to the world.
Wish not that I should compromise my penning
And scribe with the lack of feeling,
For my passion and my principles
Are the crux of my penning.
Whether the emotions they evoke
Are violent or tranquil, a smile, or a frown,
They reveal the truth of my thinking.

Ventilating with My Pen

The need to ventilate grows more and more intense
While the pressure continues to rise.
I just cannot allow the needle to reach the red zone
Because then I will be in the danger zone
Ventilating with violent combustion.

A building up of pressure that can often break a pipe.
Yearning to ventilate to circumvent my boredom
Which I suspect will soon lead to a minor depression,
If not already there. It's the same everyday monotony.
Nothing seems to change, except the days, and the nights.

When the sun retires and the moon resume its post
Searching for a way by which I can ventilate
Or circumvent the pressures that build within.
I resort to some music, and have a very limited choice.
They are not appealing and cannot soothe the savage beast.

A growing pressure that dwells within.
The problem persists and the internal combustion
Is now building momentum like a runaway train,
And the savage beast within goes wild.
With paper in hand, a pen I grip.
Then let the words flow as my cranium insists
Exposing the beast on paper, I ventilate with my pen.
That beast of its power I will now strip.

Now that beast, in submission, is kept at bay,
Slaughtered at my command with my pen if it is my wish.
I choose to keep it tamed and trained
Surrendering to my command at the tip of my pen
Which my fingers grip.

USMC Brothers

Good times and bad times we shared together
And stood by one another in our sad times,
And when it seemed too hard to endure
And wanted to shed some tears we then comforted
Each other by whispering some blissful words.

Having no mother, no father, just us, USMC
Brothers live together, love each other and
Sometimes fight for your USMC brothers,
Always knowing that we will soon be separated,
Not knowing when, where, or how.

We only share the thoughts that we will meet
Again someday. So, brothers, while we are together,
You watch my back and I'll watch yours.
Please don't catch no grenade and I won't stop no lead,
Because I can't love my brothers when they are dead.

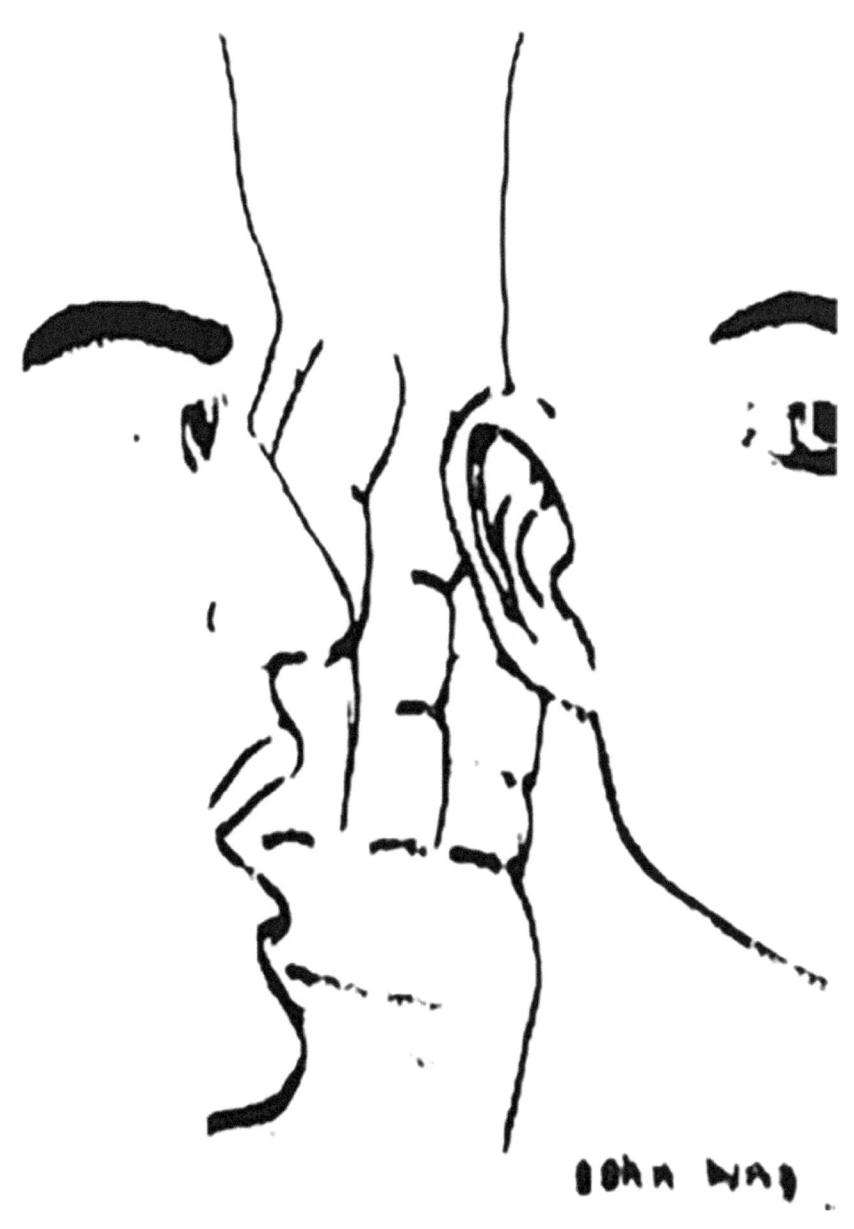

The Time Capsule: The Strides of Man

*A slow ear demands much more
Than a whispering voice is willing to give.*

A Warrior's Prayer

Dear Lord, please hear my humble plea
And help me not to hurt the innocent
I have no personal strife with my opponents.
It's unfortunate that at first we meet
On a dreaded battlefield.
Otherwise, we could have been friends.

    I merely kill to stay alive,
    So if it is alright with you, dear Lord,
    Please return me safely to my family.
    Help me to outlive my parents.
    I believe that is the way
    Life was supposed to be.

        This I ask, not merely for my sake,
        For I live by the weapons of war,
        But to spare the shattering of the hearts
        Of those who gave me life.
        But if I am asking too much of thee,
        Then be merciful when my end appears.

            And let my death be swift.
            Let me depart wearing a smile,
            Reminding the world that I hold no grudge.
            And let my body remain intact
            So that I may depart this world
            In the fashion of my birth.

A Seed of Hope

A seed of hope that was blown by a storm,
Propelled by the wind and landed on some fertile soil,
Now disburses on its own plot of ground.
There it lay at rest until the season
When nature dictate to be its home.
With the help of the rain, it germinates and blossoms
Into a beautiful flower of courage.

Then along came a most fearsome intruder.
The storm of doubt and a host of his negative friends
Intended to uproot the hope. Among his friends
Was Mr. Procrastinator, his point man,
Leading the charge with fear and neglect in close pursuit.
Then followed by sorrow and disappointment
Bringing up the rear.

Oh, how pleasant a surprise when suddenly
There appeared from nowhere missionaries of mercy.
Among the company of joy and laughter was expedience,
Leading the charge with victory and courage on their heels,
Then followed by peace, love, and harmony;
Bringing up the rear and expelling the negative forces
So that hope and courage may bloom and flourish.

My Dreamworld

Joy bells once ringing in my heart,
Now boredom is tearing it apart.
I search for some exciting ventures,
But I find them only in my sleep.
In my dreams, I have discovered a heaven,
When I lay down to rest I see vision,
While I rest and dream when I sleep,
They comfort me.

I have lived in Utopia, filled with ecstasies
Which I did fully enjoy.
In my dreams, I often fly the heights of heaven,
Exploring the universe, visiting the planets that I love,
Moving faster than the speed of light.
I speak with angels among the stars,
They pledge for peace and anti-war.

In my dreams, I navigate the oceans
And walk on their soft, sandy floors.
From the depth of the oceans,
To their surfaces, there I have traveled.
Both merman kings and mermaid queens,
We played among the reefs.
In my dreams, I visited Old England
And in Camelot, I ruled Arthur's court.

He even loaned me Excalibur,
When I rode Pegasus, to battle with Dragons.
In my dreams, I even outwitted
The legendary magician Merlin,
I roamed Sherwood Forest and saw
Cyclopes, fauns, antelopes, and unicorns.

In my dreams, I am fearless
And nothing is impossible. I walk upon water.

Swim upstream the rapids,
And climb the greatest waterfalls.
I wrestle lions, tigers, and bears.
I outrun zebras, horses, and cheetahs
In my dreams I am invincible, immortal, and never die.
Only to awake and face reality in this wretched world,
Then each night, I close my eyes with the anticipation of visiting
My dreamworld.

A Natural High

Yesterday I was intoxicated.
Without a sip of my favorite spirit.
It lasted throughout the day
With the absence of the ups and downs.
And today there is no hangover.

No drums beating in my head.
The little drummer boy
Was nowhere to be found.
No rap-a-tap-tap
Or rum-pum-pum-pum.

And so I hope
This natural high will continue,
For now, a different crave I desire,
And a higher plain I have found.
Familiar heights I have regained.

Long-lost status I have reclaimed.
My feet are unshackled, with confidence
I stride and I did not once stumble.
I stand erect with my performance at its best.
My speech coherent, I did not mumble.

The day is an excellent display
Rivaling the time of my yesteryears
When I was young, innocent, and at my best.
Yesterday I was intoxicated

And it didn't cost me one penny,
My breath was fresh
And I didn't smell like toxic fume or poison
And above all, my head was clear

And I knew that was me
So, Mr. Bartender,
Please send me the recipe
For the natural high you served me.

Again

Now I can do them much better
Because from experience I have learned
A wealth of important lessons well-earned.
Some were obtained with my time and effort.
Others, a sacrifice of blood and guts.
And on rare occasion, entrusted by destiny.

Doing it once again can sometimes,
Make it easier, especially when the first
Attempt, was not a complete disaster.
And, even then, it can be a confidence booster.
Challenge that once seemed an impossible feat,
With practice is now a walk in the park.

As I grow older and exit my teens,
I have gotten much stronger and bolder.
I even become wiser as the years roll by.
And, when I thought I had hit my peak,
I found myself pleasantly surprised
When I realized I was still doing better.

Even when I thought it was impossible,
A mortal can do no more, again I surprise myself,
Now I am forced to raise the bar even higher.
The Sky has no limit; some things just get better,
And so I place no restrictions on myself
And accept the fact that practice becomes perfect.

Aged

Searching the brain to free some thought;
Thought that age has held as captive
Now need a ransom to be free;
Thoughts that are trapped in the subconscious
And refuse to surface to the conscious now.

    Thoughts that were often used for many years
    Now almost forgotten when needed fast.
    They are so difficult to surface quickly on demand,
    Unlike in our youthful years past
    When we were fresh and green as grass.

Thoughts that jump from subconscious to conscious;
So fast, and filled with enthusiasm,
Like they were popping corn.
Dare those youthful thoughts then
To ever being contained.

    But now with the passing of time
    They are being held as captive.
    Now we have to search very diligently,
    Sometimes only to find them tangled by our age.

Ahead

Is there really a past remaining behind us?
Can we go back and take a peep
Or do we take it with us to mold today
As a part of our evolution?
Or is the past just a mere figment of our mind
Just one long continuing process?

When the seconds advance to minutes,
And minutes turns to hours,
Then continues to a day,
Then a week, a month, and a year…
Then that which we deemed the past
Is composed into the now and eternity.

Do we ever leave them behind us?
Or just compound to be a larger part
The past, the present, and the future?
Without events, can they be distinguished
From the monotony of the rising of the sun
To the never changing of its setting,

Always moving from the east to the west
Predictable is its path
Yet mystifying in its intent.
If not for the sake of light and darkness,
The never-changing night and day
All would remain the same
Except the shape of the moon.

Can time be differentiated
Without an event?
Time capsule play by its own rule
No one knows the contents of its core,
Then what is time, this question I ask?
The answer is locked in the time capsule.

Among Us

Stand on my back so you too
Can rise when I rise, he proclaimed.
He was overwhelmed with emotion,
The well of his eyes were overflowing,
And tears trickled down his cheeks.

He stood erect and proud, exhibiting a man,
And made no excuses for his emotion,
Jesus wept. And so should man.
And no one dared to dispute
A genuine moment that personifies his emotion.

The depth of concern for his fellow man
Created the standard
By which brotherhood should be held,
A moment when selfishness
Was sacrificed and laid to rest.

And the true love for humanity
Had surfaced at its best.
Mortals who possess those characteristics
Lead while others follow,
And as an emblem they wear a white collar.

To make obvious what they represent.
Thanks to the *Almighty*
For those among us you sent.
Blessed with meekness and compassion,
Whose traits soften our hearts of stone.

Angels

There are some messengers called angels,
Be not misled, they are both good and bad,
There are those that are loyal to the creator,
And those that are faithful to the devil.
Though the light overcomes the darkness.

The darkness still exists in its dormant stage
Waiting for the light to depart so it can return.
Thanks to the light for keeping the darkness at bay.
Angels are among us; we see them everywhere.
Like mortals, we can never tell who they really are.

When tedious tasks are being performed around us
Those we thought were impossible, if not angels, then who?
Who then, or what, could solve that mystery?
And then, when unexplainable tragedies occur,
Who is to be blamed, if not the angel of darkness?

Angels are with us. They make the impossible possible.
Sometimes, they appear in the form of a human,
And other times, they appear in the spirit world.
We call their actions miracles, when good deeds are done,
And when the devil is in play, then call it what they may.

As Romans Do

We visited Rome and fell in love with it.
And so, slowly but surely,
We began to adopt the Romans ways
And we made Rome our home,
Oh, how soon we forsake African ways,
We became gladiators by slaying our brothers.

Every adult no longer a parent
For each child in the village,
For Rome has no village.
When we became citizens of Rome
We abandoned our locks and braids
And picked up the curling irons and the wigs.

We conquered and destroyed the innocent,
And we gave their possessions to Rome,
Our Nubian Queens, their virtue stolen,
And our kings, defended their lives in the arena
To entertain the aristocrats of Rome.
When you are in Rome, and do as Romans do.

Then you have failed to be a Daniel
And stand for the principles
In which you believe,
Unlike our forefathers who refuse
To sing songs of Zion to those
Who had carried them away captive
As they wept, by the River of Babylon.

The Time Capsule: The Strides of Man

*They who have no feet to dance
Must dance, from within their heart.*

A Sailor's Plight

A Phantom ship, or some seafarer's myth
This marooned sailor was thinking
As he traveled along the shore
Looking for the highest peak with the tallest tree
To make his lookout post.
From there he could watch the horizon
For any vessel that might appear.

A phantom ship a-sailing
'Twas only a poor, lonely sailor's wish
This marooned sailor alone, yelling,
Come now and rescue me!
For unless my eyes are now deceiving me
A ship I see appearing
With the sails all filled with the wind.
Now it's bursting through the fog.

A phantom ship he had caught a glimpse.
But as he gazed and gazed with constancy,
No ship had ever arrived.
I have seen such ships before, he pondered,
As vivid as I glimpse just now,
With merman kings, mermaids, and seahorses
All on deck, dancing up a spree.

A phantom ship played a trick on him.
Or could it be that his lonesome self
Tried to entertain him, or to delude him
Or perhaps, just a lonely mind with too much time.
In the absence of any other of his kind,
Illusion creeps in to occupy his mind
And he saw a phantom ship that never existed.

Atlantic

Plains boats and ships to the great Atlantic,
They are all the same,
An ocean gigantic and deep.
There lies miles and miles to the other side,
A fearsome journey you must realize.
Thus many vessels have capsized.
Novices, mediocrities, and experts…
Some never made it to their berth.

As the legend of the Greeks proclaim,
The long-lost Kingdom of Atlantis
Made the great Atlantic ocean floor
It's forever famous watery home.
Venture me with caution please,
Because sometimes my anger I must release
Especially in the winter.

On my northern side be extremely cautious.
This is when my tempest most often
Grows very cold and wild.
With massive waves of watery mountains
Tumbling like the Victoria Falls.
No wonder many vessels lay at rest
On the awesome Atlantic ocean floor—
Merchants, fisherman, Navy and the Marines—
I bid you all caution to take.

Captains, pilots, mates, and crew,
They all call mid-Atlantic the point of no return,
When he is calm and resting.
Or even motionless while sleeping,
Enjoy my stillness and fear no wrong.

Or when I awaken from my slumber and its galling
Your chances you may take, it is safe to say
No harm will befall you then.

But when I am angry and in a rage
And my surface is all white, that's the time
When my anger I must release
Then for heaven's sake, venture not
Or you may forever rest on my ocean floor.

My Children

My poems are my children,
Presented in the form of words.
Please don't ask me which is my favorite,
I love them all and favor them.

For different reasons,
Yet I love them equally.
If I am forced to make one a sacrifice,
Such a price I could not pay.

The characters they play,
Makes each child unique in their own way.
Some are bold and fearless,
With no bridles on their tongues.

Their words are uncoached, unpolished,
And raw, from their lips.
The way eager children are.
Freely outspoken,

Expressing a mind of their own,
Unrestricted words, spewing freely
Like water sprouting from a fountain,
Pure and fresh from the earth's core.

Or flowing like the river Nile
To the Mediterranean Sea,
Drenching all its contact, along the way
For their free-spirit, I love them best.

There are also those of my children,
Who are timid and shy.
Frequently they hold back
And think twice before they speak.

They are the meek,
Oh so gentle, kind, and sweet,
Never wanting to offend,
Always trying their best to please.

And live by the creed.
Soft words deter wrath,
While harsh and grieving words
Invite anger.

Always in control of their emotions,
knowing they are the masters of their faith,
For those characteristics, I love them best.
They inherit my heart.

There are others of my children
Who are rebellious, challenging, and wild.
They live by a different code of conduct.
Blood for blood,

A pound of flesh or a pint of blood,
Each vendetta they must settle,
With no regard of the cost.
A score or a century, all is fair.

Blood for blood, they will settle
A payment for a family or a friend,
And they too I love best.

For the warriors they are,
With their unsurrendering fighting spirit,
A day of reckoning they pledge to see.

My Late Pen

It is late into my evenings,
Soon my shadow will begin to fall.
I have no time to rest my fingers,
Even though they are growing weary.
Now a lifetime of experience
Gathered over my many mornings,
With just a few evenings remaining
In which I hope to pen them.
I have found my pen
Late into the eve of my life.
I wished I had found it
In my early morn, or at noon
When I was at my best.
Nevertheless, I will accept
My late evening finding anyway
And pray that it is not too late.
It is better late rather than not at all.
I have found my late pen
And now, with the world I am sharing
My hopes, my thoughts, and my life,
From a fading memory, and my late-found pen.
I have found my pen in the evening of my life,
When my vision begins to diminish
And my light is no longer brightly shining.
In my evening, when those who gave birth
And nurtured me have already departed
Without the opportunity to read my writing,
As the evening of my day draws nigh.
Nevertheless, life is not too cruel after all.
My successors will read my penning.
Now I ponder, will the ink in my pen be suffice,
And if not, do I have a fountain

From which I can refill,
Or do I have the luxury of time?
No more questions of my destiny,
I will just scribe my pen and let it be.
Before my night appears,
I hope I will have ample time
To state my story, before I lay my pen down
And the dark shadows fall upon me.
Though I wish I had found my pen at dawn,
With youth and years before me, I sincerely say
It is better late than never.

Listen to New York

Have you ever listened to New York?
If not, I am inviting you to listen.
You will find yourself pleasantly surprised
With its many sounds;
From the bellowing sound of the Niagara's fall
At our northern border
To the southern shores of Staten Island.

Blasting the whistle of the ferries
Along the eastern tip of Montauk.
The sound of waves crashing on its rocks
Or rolling its blanket or foam across the sand,
Mimicking the sound of dry leaves
Tossed by the wind in Prospect Park Brooklyn.

Or on the western hills of Chautauqua,
whistling pines, and weeping willows.
The howling wind over the Catskill Mountains
That echoes in the valleys below
And in the realm of its four corners.
There are interesting sounds to enjoy.

Listen to the fire engines blasting their sirens
On their way to rescue someone,
The ambulance rushing to introduce
A new life, or even to prolong one.
There is also the sound of the police
Whose siren is always unpredictable.
Sometimes they are on their way to save life,
And other times to take life

Listen to New York, the rumbling of
The trains at 149th Street and Third Avenue.
You will be able to tell the difference
Between the 2 and the 5 train blindfolded,
How the number 2 glides smoothly through
While the number 5 with noise laboriously
Screeching around the bend.

Listen to the performers
At Grand Central Station,
Or those on the subway platform.
Listen to New York in the morning.
You may find a pleasant greeting.
Good Day, New York.

Keeper of the City

Adorned in their royal blue attire
And most of their hearts are royal too
While in constancy they rolled the dice
By putting their lives constantly on the line.
Most of them, if given the chance to know,
You will find them to have a heart like yours.

Yes, undeniably there are those few
Who have defiled the royal blue attire
And tarnished the principle for which it stands.
With the hateful intention, they performed
Their homicidal ventures, or even those
Who are abusive with their power.

Regrettably there are some unwritten laws
By which they make their pact to secrecy
Thus impeding us of a fair play and transparency.
Now the task at hand for those who are in charge
To protect and serve, is to break the vow of silence
And abolish the nonexistent quota, as they claim.

But fret not yourself because of the few evildoers.
Their day of reckoning one day will come.
And this I beg of you to remember;
That the vast majority that wears the royal blue
Do have a heart like yours, and a family too,
And are human with emotions just like you.

The keeper of the city adorned in their royal blue,
And most of them are loyal to the cause they choose
To protect and to serve the city they love.
Bear this in mind; where there is no law
The people are bound to perish.
What would a city be like without the police?

Christmas for Two by the Fire

It's Christmas time, joy bells are ringing
From every house you can hear carols singing,
Wreaths, stars, and mistletoes are hanging,
And on every door, lights are blinking
While the smell of gingerbread is in the air.
Christmas is here again.

It's winter, and it's cold outside.
The ground is all covered with snow,
The roofs are fashioned with their white blankets
And the trees look like
They are wrapped with cotton balls.

The branches are all laden,
Waiting for the slightest rush of wind to fall,
The kids are all playing,
Some are sleighing
Others are sliding and free-falling.
Let's celebrate this Christmas inside.
I will start the fire
While you get the marshmallows
And we can both dress like Santa Claus
You will be Mrs. Claus
And I will be Mr. Claus.

Let's hang lots of mistletoe,
Sit and watch the fire glow,
And when it's time to exchange gifts,
Let's start with a kiss
Sitting by our fireplace
Having a wonderful Christmas tonight.

Stolen by the Master

And when they could no longer be concealed
By binding with cloth
Torn from the hem of her mother's dress.
A desperate maternal attempt to elude,
The inquisitive roaming eyes
Of the so-called master on the prowl
For his next victim,
Who dares to approach puberty.

It now becomes apparent,
That the disguise could no longer concealed,
The flourishing pair of plums
That were kept inside,
And now protruding its restraint.
Thus was forced to be abandoned and cast aside,
Revealing beauty and innocence
Borne by a Nubian child.

As the so-called master's perverted mind wanders wild
And his inquisitive stalking eyes roam the fields,
He beholds the forbidden fruit,
Naive and innocent, not yet fit to be plucked
Below a pair of gleaming eyes and curly black hair,
Perched upon an innocent virgin chest,
Like a pair of miniature pyramids at sunset's rest,
Those plums her mother diligently bound to conceal.

Now with a menacing pedophile smile,
He wags his tongue in a serpentlike fashion
And of the mother, he demanded
"Tonight, you will bring your daughter to my barn
And let the house servants have her properly adorned."

But like any loving mother, she declined,
Knowing she had just made an appointment with his cat-o-nine.
Soon in public, she is being displayed.

Bounded to the flogging pole,
With the rope from the so-called master's favorite mount.
"Twenty-one lashes from the cat-o-nine
For as long as you refuse to comply
With that command of mine.
I am lord and master of these fields
Thus I make claim to all that is produced upon it.

Mortal or immortal, mine to pluck as I deem fit
And this maiden that I desire.
There should be no objection or denial
Master's horse, master's grass."
Another virgin, the so-called master has stolen.

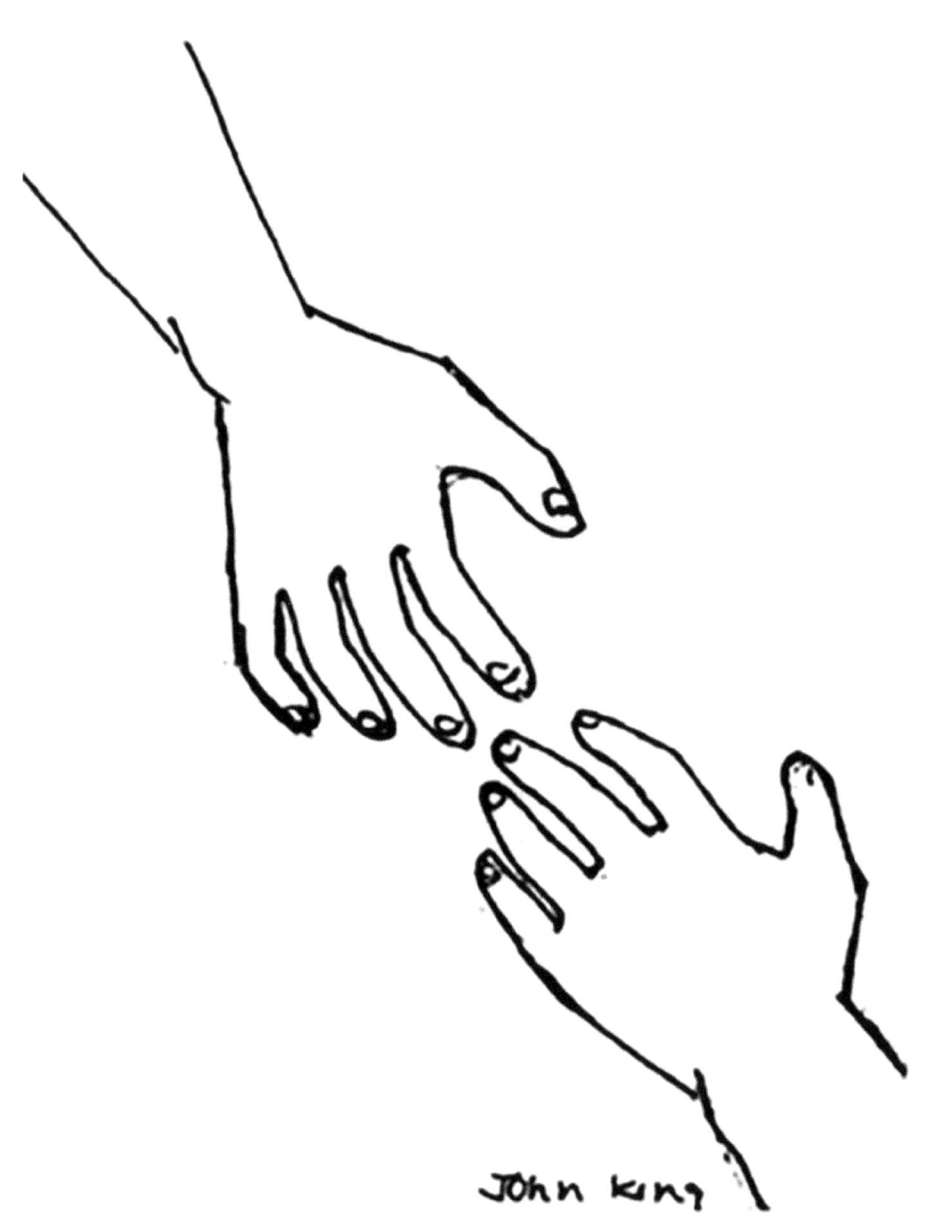

NORMAN W. SMITH

*Being brave when acting for yourself
Is the will to remain alive;
But being brave for others is called humane.*

Master Rooster

Celebrating the battle he had won,
Cock-co-reek-coo, Cock-co-reek-coo
He chants and crows his song.
Cock-co-reek-coo as he continues
His proud victory dance.

Covered with blood and ruffled feathers,
Wearing the scars.
He had fought a brilliant fight;
One last grandstand to entertain his fans,
Leaving no doubt,
Who is the master in that barn.

All these chicks you see,
I am the father of them all,
His opponent with both eyes closed
Staggering and falling incoherently and blind,
He had lost his vision in the fight.
His wings are hanging by his side.

Just too worn or probably broken,
They can't be tucked inside.
If only he had run,
He could live to fight another day,
But instead death awaits him
In such a painful way.

While the victor mounts on his stump,
Flapping his wings and beating on his chest,
Showboating to the hens,
That he is the master of the barn,

Cock-co-reek-coo, cock-co-reek coo
He crows his song in triumph.

Tonight I will roost and rest,
Nurse my aching wounds,
And be back at dawn
Still crowing my song
Cock-co-reek-coo, cock-co-reek-coo
For I am the master of my barn.

Starting Over

The race is not over
Because you have failed.
Ahead lies many miles
Still remaining to go.

Some may say that
It is harder starting over,
While others will say that it is easier.
You have done most of it before.

You may not know exactly
Just where you should go,
But there is one thing you know for sure.
You know where not to go.

Starting over does show
That you are courageous,
Ambitious, and proud,
And that you are not willing
To accept an obstacle as being defeated.

Accept no failures,
But try to understand them,
Because by accepting failure
You may soon compromise your integrity
And begin to accept defeat.

The only time you really fail
Is when you refuse to try.
And in your trying, embrace faith.
It weighs much more than you may think.

Because practice makes perfect,
Each time you try and do not succeed
You have not failed.
Instead, you have gained the practice
To achieve perfection.

While striving to achieve success,
Cultivate being an optimist.
That will increase your faith,
Keeping in mind that faith and optimism
Are twins working together.

The Spices of Life

You then think of the bees and thank the little creatures
For their service and the immense pleasure they offer.
While life tends to be good to us, our gratitude we give.

But not all the spices of life are pleasant in their taste,
For when the bee is upset and pierces you with its sting,
You no longer give your gratitude, but smite it if you can.
No one can certainly say the flavor dictates the mood.

When upon your lips lay the sweet taste of your honey's lips,
You then think of the birds and the bees and of life's bliss,
And you're thankful for the pleasure that love brings with it.
Love is the most intense fragrance among our spices of life.

The unpleasant spices of life we must not forget, such as Envy and jealousy. They represent the bitter and the sour. Their skunk-like smell and disgusting taste; do avoid them. Acquire a better taste, appreciating the wondrous spices
Of life.

The Earth

The Earth is the Lord's,
And his fullness manifests in man.
Thus from his flesh, the earth,
We were molded into his image,
And from his vineyard
We have been plucked free
And granted his love to suckle
On the grapes of his vine,
To tread upon his earth,
His flesh and his footstool.

All the waters of this land,
The ocean, sea, lakes, rivers, and ponds,
They are his veins, his arteries,
And his capillaries through which
The substance of our life, the waters flow.
Red juice from his grapes, like his blood,
Upon which we suckled by his love,
Plucked from the vine attached to his loins,
The blessed earth, from which we were molded.
And from his throne up above.

He looks down with his tender love,
And with mercy he cries, shedding
His tears of rain to soften his flesh
To prepare the soil for his vineyard of red grapes.
Grapes, upon which we suckle
To make the fluid that flows through our veins
Now runs until death to thy flesh we return.

Awful Nights

Oh, how weird a sight when the light grows dim
And hides itself from the awful deeds of the night,
When creeps and freaks come out in full display
And hell lets loose its vagrant occupants to loot,
When good takes a rest and evil parasites plunder.

Oh, how tranquil a night, when most of the world
Is asleep in bliss as the light hides and ceases to gleam,
And blindness is naive while evil reigns supreme,
In the blackness of the night as the light goes to rest
And evil finds a paradise to roam without a threat.

Oh, how good a sight to see when the morn returns,
As the devils and their evil flee from the light of day.
Now in wrath the devil curses the light for its return
And the fowl deeds must cease as the dawn appears.
Then let the night and the day exchange their places.

Oh, how good at last when we see the lights return.
While the night regrets the coming of the morning
For with the dawn the world is awakened to see
The beauty of the sun's glittering rays beaming down.

Barack Obama

Sing, O minstrel, sing of our history,
    For he was born of a lowly birth,
        Bred with the charms and quality of nobility.
            Who then would dare to say, noble parents
                Would not have wished to bear such a son?

Many temptations must have come his way,
    And likewise arrows tried to pierce his dream.
        Nevertheless, with his true fortitude,
            He refused to sway
                And kept his eyes fastened on the prize.

If our first president, George Washington,
    Was given the title of a King,
        Then Barack Obama
            Would be wearing a crown today.
                Oh, how I wish to lift my voice and sing
                    Praises to Barack Hussein Obama
                        In the highest office of the land.

Sing, O minstrel, sing your ballad to the world
    As we continue to write our history,
        For Obama has joined the ranks,
            That of an elected king
                With the only absence of
                    His crown and his throne.

Sing, O minstrel, sing of the changes
    That we have made,
        For the height Obama has attained
            Has proven that we are near
                In accepting a man for his ability
                    Irrespective of the color of their skin.

And when we get there
    We can then reminisce
        On Douglass, Tubman, King, and the rest
            Of the struggle from the cotton field
                To the position of elected king.

Wounded Wings

It was a splendid autumn evening.
The air was fresh and the sky
Was cloudless and bright.
An exciting evening for an excursion flight,
When a tragic turn of events
Gloomed the afternoon.

A dove in flight at the brink of death
Escaped with its life
From the claws of a falcon, for its folly.
Now with wounded wings,
Overcome with pain it could no longer bear
And took refuge in the canopy
Of a great old red oak tree
To rest and heal its wings.

As days went by and things got worse,
The dove now realized
It was unable to fly and useless to try.
A lonely falcon came cruising by
And was invited in
For a meal to share.
With skillful maneuver the falcon abruptly
Circled and entered in
And was surprised to see a lonely dove
To welcome him in.

Once more our paths have crossed
My clumsy guest
I hope by now your skill you have improved.
There is a meal to be served
But no one with whom to share.

The Gallows

Ticktock, ticktock, ticktock, ticktock.
The inaudible sound of the clock
Embedded in his mind.
It appears to be deafening
As his time was slowly counting down,
As the hour grows close for him
To step upon the gallows
And hang by the neck until he is dead.

The price he was sentenced to pay
When in a drunken rage
A priest he slaughtered and laid to rest.
A fatal bullet he planted to his victim's chest.
The priest he shot wore a pistol for hunting
And to keep at bay wild animals of prey,
But never intended a human life to take.

No one seems to fathom
The depth of the unfortunate incident,
Was it a deliberate malicious act,
Or pure alcoholic madness?
Whatever the form or cause,
An innocent life he had robbed.

The inaudible sound of a deafening clock
Goes rampant in his mind.
He seems to be wild and insane,
He seems to be losing his mind.
He never stood still,
Constantly pacing the cell.

The bald spots on both sides of his head
Remain constantly swollen
From bashing his head on the wall.
And every Sunday when the church bell tolls
He takes his hands, covers his ears,
And folds into a fetal position.
Other times he clasps his hands and falls
To his torn and tattered knees to pray.

It is fast-approaching six months
Since he was sentenced to be hanged
Within one hundred and eighty days
Of his judgment,
And he has been counting down ever since.
Now the thought weighs heavily on his mind.
The last week seems like a thousand years
And the last day like ten thousand,
The days were getting longer,
And now the last hour seems to be eternity.

It took him just a fraction of a second
To retrieve his six-shooter from the holster
As the victim fell to the ground.
They say he was the fastest in the west.
It shows an irony to the tyrant
When time stood still
As he stepped upon the gallows
And bid the world farewell.

NORMAN W. SMITH

*Best friends make a lasting and desirable
Companion, in addition a unique relationship.*

Warriors' Mothers

Warriors' mothers, with bleating voices they plead
Return to us intact, the fruits of our womb.
When their children are deployed
Off to some strange, distant land to war,
Countless sleepless nights
In their hearts they ponder
Where are our wondering warriors tonight?
Sleep never comes easy.
Torment and fear appears to be
The normal order of the restless nights.
Addiction often becomes their only relief,
Be it prescribed or self-imposed,
Dependency frequently presides.

Warriors' mothers, who infrequently get to rest,
In their sleep they are tormented by nightmares,
And haunting dreams,
And while they are awake, they are tortured
Constantly by memories of pictures
Hanging on the walls,
Notches and marks of pens, crayons, and pencils.
As their size increases over the years
To the point where they are fully grown,
And off to the war, they are gone.

Dusty bikes inside the garage,
Their favorite mittens, balls, bats, and hats,
All displayed on a shelf.
The school around the corner
Gives a constant reminder
Each time they pass by
Of the warriors mothers bore

And those who paid the ultimate price;
Their life for their country, they sacrifice.
Warriors' mothers with bleating voices,
They too pay tremendously.
When the fruits of their womb are laid silently in a tomb,
Laboring pains revisit them mimicking the day of birth,
Agonies I am sure only mothers dare to fathom.
And grief no tears can relieve.
As a veteran and a parent, with deepest sincerity I truly say,
My heart cries out in sympathy
For warriors' mothers, in a very special way.

DWI Victims

White bikes on public display
Scattered over our city,
Especially at the intersections,
Indicating that a child was killed
Somewhere in its proximity,
Robbed of their life and liberty,
Deprived of the God-promised opportunity,
A command from our creation
To go forth and multiply.
Some never had a chance
To fulfill that command.
They left us in their infancy.

Never had a sweet-sixteen birthday party,
Or even attended their high school prom.
White bikes on the streets served as landmarks
Where a child had been slain,
But surely there are many others who were cut down
And there are no reminders.
Some selfish, gluttonous drunken driver
Had robbed another innocent soul, and what makes
These thoughtless, selfish acts so unbearable
They all could and should have been avoided.
The young, the old, and those in between
Are all victims of DWI.

The dead, the maim and the kinfolk
That remain endured the brutal torture
That scarred their wounded hearts,
The little girls and boys
Who shared their rooms with their siblings,
And possibly their beds as well,
With indescribable regrets and torturous nights.

They, with vigor, fight to remain sane
When the familiar voices are absent
And someone made their life a living hell.

A selfish, gluttonous drunken driver
Had cast his spell on them.
When in solitude they lay,
Perplexed and angry for their loss,
Their wounded hearts no time to heal,
Involuntarily reflect on their next of kin.
The selfish, gluttonous drunken driver
From them did steal
The joy and happiness the times
With their loved ones would reveal.

When it was time to play,
With their imaginations
They wandered from their room
And traveled over the globe
As their rooms transformed to castles
While playing kings and queens,
Or using their sheets and pitching tents
As they camped on the plains of Africa,
Or even on Mount Everest's peak.
Wherever their imagination took them,
There they would roam
Now that their other half is gone.

And they, like prisoners in their haunted rooms,
Grandmothers who used to bake and shop for two,
Find themselves with excess
When they briefly forgot that some selfish,
Gluttonous drunken driver did rob her of one.
Preschoolers, teenagers, adolescents,
Adults, grandparents, and great-grandparents,
We all share in common the burden of victims
Robbed by selfish, gluttonous drunken drivers.

Polly and the Bee

My dear little bumblebee
I am awfully sorry for scaring you
And I must be blamed for your death.
It is really tearing me apart
And I can't cease from crying.
You looked quite lovely
Dressed in your yellow and black stripes.

Always moving from flower to flower.
My teacher told me you are working
To make our garden grow flowers and fruits.
I watch you for hours
And you never stop to take a break.
I only tried to touch you
To hear your buzzing sound.

And though your sting
Caused me a great deal of pain,
I am sorry you had to die.
But I didn't mean to scare you,
And I didn't know that if you stung me, you would die.
But I will tell your siblings or children
To visit my garden without fear,
And I will never try again to touch them.

Fred

He was witty, charming and funny,
Thus combining those envied qualities
Made him great to be around
And even his more impressive traits
he had never entertained a single foe,
Always friends wherever he goes.

Seldom, if ever, was he sad,
And even rarer to see him mad.
He was never warlike, seeking strife,
But if he could have cheated death
I know he would have a gallant fight
To the very end.

It seems he never had a fighting chance
Because destiny had played well its part
And captured him far before his prime,
About three years short of twenty-one,
A trifling gain for a terrific loss.
I shed my tears and bid my friend farewell
Knowing now God has a better plan for Fred.

Hunting the Hunter

A hunter lay down
In his cabin to rest,
Exhausted from the tiresome night
He had spent stalking a deer.
The buck he shot
Still hanging from his beam.

Already skinned and quartered.
He was fatigued from the many hours
He had spent tracking this buck.
His watchful Irish hound
And faithful Labrador retriever
Now torn to pieces.

While attempting to stop a grizzly
From entering his door.
In the commotion, he was awakened,
Only to find himself facing an angry bear
That was now stalking him.

Beginning from the spot
Where he had made his kill,
He methodically
Pulled an arrow from his quiver
And strung his bow,
Aimed patiently with skill.

He gently let the arrow go.
It found its mark and fastened well,
Pierced through his heart,
The buck fell dead.
It was from there the trail of blood begins,
And ended at his cabin door.

Where an angry, stalking grizzly stood.
Now that the hunter
Is being hunted and confronted,
Will there be another killing?
Of man or beast?

Lost Valentine

Each year a mysterious flower
Bloomed in a village square
Just before Valentine's Day.
It was the most beautiful flower
Anyone have ever seen.
In all the world around
No one have ever seen its likeness,
And no one knows
How it got there, or its name
And so the town was named Valentine.

Faithfully the flower bloomed
Each year just before Valentine's Day,
And so visitors would gather
From miles and miles around
To behold the beauty in splendor rare.
Artists with their canvas
All laid out on easels,
Photographers with their cameras,
All in an effort to duplicate
This mysterious flower,
A splendor in Valentine's square.

A magnificent spectacle
And a joy for everyone,
Birds, bees, and other insects too.
It was the landmark of the village,
And their pride upon which to bask and boast
Upon each Valentine's Day,
Selfishness imposed upon this dear lad.
The prettiest flower he has ever seen,
A fitting present for my dearest
on this Valentine's Day.

As his selfishness persisted,
From the stalk he plucked the flower,
So deep in the ground that flower
Would never bloom again.
Thus everyone lost
Their beautiful splendor, oh so rare,
The spectacle of the town.
And so they made a creed
Never to celebrate Valentine's ever again
And renamed the town Lost Valentine.

Natural Beauty

Nature has been very kind to me today
As she entreated my eyes to feast on beauty,
Natural beauty in its purest form
As naked as a rose, or any other flower
And just as beautiful and attractive.

Her hair was black and curly gleaming in the sun
No sign of chemically treated
It seems just naturally from her birth
She was just as beautiful and attractive.
My words do her an injustice
When I attempt to describe her beauty.

When my eyes upon this fair maiden fell,
I stood aghast and gluttonously feasted my eyes,
But yet to satisfy my intimate prayer.
Though she was dressed in simple garment,
She outclassed all else in view.
In fact, she was the cloak that covered them all.

The Shepherd's Light

A perilous night on a stormy sea
No moon or stars were there to see.
The sky was black as the shepherd's coal
That which he used to fuel his fire.
A ship adrift with the crew in despair
When lightning rips the dark night air
Revealing a dim speck of light.

They piled inside their lifeboat
And headed toward the glow.
Soon they found a shepherd's cottage without a door.
Good shepherd, can we enter in?
The shepherd replied, it is for that reason
Why I hang no door
I am a shepherd for men, my flocks are my company.

Over the years, numerous souls I have saved,
And I have shed likewise as many tears
For those that I could not aid.
See that grove over yonder,
As far as your eyes can see
I have planted a tree for each corpse
That washed upon this shore.

And from those trees, I have burned the coal
To fuel this flame that rescued you.
Then let us build a lighthouse,
One that towers toward the sky
And shines its beams for miles around
That we can be its keeper, and a shepherd too.

*If not thy mysteries to let us understand
Then help us, dear Lord, that we may obey
Your commandments.*

Markings of Time

Nature leaves with us
Its markings of time
That we may count the years
Or the centuries as they roll by.
In many ways, it makes an almanac,
Writing our history with its signs.

When our yesteryear has vanquished,
Nature slowly dispenses information
As time leaves its mark in our history;
Stalagmite hanging in ancient caves,
Fossils embedded deeply in the rocks,
Telling our history in layers of the earth.

Oil, coal, diamonds, and other minerals,
The time capsule releases its clues,
Rings in the cores of trees
And around their barks
Where Mother Nature
Leaves her markings of time.

The silverback gorilla,
The leader of his pack,
And the gray-haired old man
Relaxing in his rocking chair
Amusing his grandchildren,
Displaying the markings of time.

The smooth stones in our path
On which we constantly trod,
The rocks in the ravine,
Or those in the damp banks of canyons
All covered with thick green moss;
Nature saying no one trod upon them.

The Indian's Plight

It was the year of fourteen hundred and ninety-two
When the, Nina, the Pinta, and the Santa Maria
Invaded the contented and peaceful Caribbean shore
'Twas that day the devil went knocking
On their heavenly door.

Soon the exploitation of the Arawak Indian began as slaves,
And within one hundred years of Spain's plundering
The Arawak Indians were now doomed to extinction.
They came, they plundered, and soon
They will make an end.

What was once the peaceful Caribbean shores
Now stained with the blood of the innocent Arawak Indians
Who were often decapitated, merely for entertainment,
To see who with one blow could sever an Indian's head
Closest to the victim's shoulder.

And while several swords were broken in such barbaric acts,
Frequent weeping and wailing for heads that were severed.
The three Spanish ships Columbus landed in the Caribbean
Planted their havoc and annihilation
The Arawak Indians did reap.

The Eskimo Hunter

The winter storm came swift and hard.
A hunter stranded far from his village,
His sleigh was heavily laden from a successful hunt
Stacked with deer, elk, caribou, and seals.
The thick snow formed a wall all around him,
He himself was covered with inches of snow.
His Huskies now looked like polar bears,
Too tired to shake off the relentless snow.
He stopped and built himself a camp
To rest until the storm subsided.
But days and nights now look the same,
No celestial body to use as his guide.

No Sun, no moon, no stars could he see,
Nothing from above with rays or beams
To penetrate the white blanket of snow
That refused to stop from pouring down.
His tent now an igloo all covered with snow,
Billions of little flakes dancing to the ground.
To him his world now is just a white dome,
Stranded and bare, just him and his dogs.
Soon the villagers will be starving,
Thus he must continue his journey home.
And so he sat and chatted with his dogs
As if they were having a council meeting.

My life and the lives of all the villagers
Are now completely on your backs.
Every now and then they would wag their tails,
Raise their ears or give a passive growl
As if to say they all understand.
Soon you will have to find your way home

Through this dense wall of falling snow.
Right then his lead dog rose to its feet
Sniffing the air and prancing about,
Then he barked and gave his command,
And all the rest were up and about.
He harnessed them and headed homeward bound.

The Casted Lot

The Roman soldiers cast their lots
For a purple robe.
Whosoever the lot fell upon
Would win that precious and envied robe.

Upon us lowly creatures a casted lot
Of colors was assigned,
But much unlike the Roman soldiers
We were given no choice of our lot,
A design by nature entrusted upon us.

And while in our stride to reach the top,
To some it becomes a stumbling block.
Many dark days indelibly blot our history.
The Jews, they suffered their holocaust,
And like nomads they wandered,
Seeking an acceptable existence.

The native Indians of the new world
Had more than their share of suppression.
Some tribes were completely annihilated,
While others were driven to the brink of extinction
As the old world of Europe infringed
Upon their contented way of life.

Yet impossible to forget the atrocity
That was cast upon the dark-skinned man.
Penned in our history as the triangular trade,
Brutally uprooted from his homeland,
Brutally transported to the new world.
Brutally he was forced to labor
And brutally many were slaughtered.

What if we all were of one race?
What if we give peace a chance?
Would not this world be a better place?
What if we all try to let it be.

Village Child

Somewhere back in time,
When a village used to raise a child,
Before tradition lost its value,
And our children began to spoil,
When children respected every adult
And every adult acted as a mother or a father
To every child.

Somewhere back in time,
When children did not put aside
The teachings of their homes
And roam wild because their parents were not in sight,
When it was each adult's duty
To mold and scold each child,
Every man and woman in those villages was a parent
To every child.

Somewhere back in time,
Parents were deprived of their control,
Asking where did we go wrong?
Was it from the villages to the cities?
Or from our city halls to our home's walls?
Where we were forced from our teachings
Of biblical times, and now spared the rod to
Spoil the child.

Life

Created obscurely in the womb,
A small, dark, and sometimes, a lonely room
Lucky if you are a twin, a triplet, or sometimes more
Then you will foster unbreakable bonds of kinship.
Friends for life will be personified
And loneliness will be vanquished at its birth.

And now the time has come
To depart from the sheltered fortress of the womb,
Ejected by Mother Nature, a term we call birth.
And as nature's cycle miraculously evolves
And its marvelous mysteries unfold,
Delivering its long-anticipated package at last.

Relinquishing its small, dark, and often-lonely room.
And when the eyes at first behold the world,
Was it joy or horror an infant felt,
Was our senses then too faint to tell,
Or could it be that emotions
Were simply unknown.

Now cast into this tempestuous sea of life,
Tossed by billows of temptation, strife, and woes
No longer sheltered in the fortress of the womb
Ejected by Mother Nature,
The term we called birth.
No more dark and sometimes lonely room.

We have instead a grave possibility
Of being a tomb
With hungry, vicious predator
Waiting to seize the moment
To capitalize on the vaguest of mistake,
Slaughtering and plundering to make an end.

Crucial moments we now experience.
No time for mistakes or to procrastinate,
Embrace with vigor the joys of life around you
And live each day as if it is your last.
Life is short and death is sure.
Have no fear of the tomb or dying,
For both are mere bridges to a higher plateau,
The afterlife utopia.

After All

After all the words we have spoken
Starting from the beginning of time
There remains some still unspoken
New words approaching every day.

After all the records that has broken
The process remains a constant one
New records keep broken each day
As our strides continue along our way.

After all the stories that's being told
Both the amazing and the tragic ones
Still there remain oh so many stories
The ears have yet to receive.

After all the places that we have gone
Mingled and roamed among the stars
To the moon and contemplating Mars
There are still infinite places remaining.

After all our desires silent and subliminal
Places which our soles have yet to trod
All that us simple mortals have attained
After all, we have only just began.

An Empty Chair

An empty chair that bears no weight
It has no influence upon one's view
But when it is occupied it becomes
A spectacle and influences everyone
That falls within its realm.

An empty throne within a palace
With a scepter remains unraised
The prince must fit his father's shoe
And wear that vacant crown
His kingdom now for him to reign.

An empty chair within iron bars
Its lever had just been pulled
The courtyard is filled with mourners
All dressed in black and teary eyes
Its last occupant had just resigned.

Perhaps to hell dare one to say
But for now his corps will lie at rest
Upon boot hill among lilacs and lilies
Were there too many empty chairs?
Could he have chosen the wrong chair?

Ancient Man

An ancient man, who knew nothing more
Than to labor only with his bare hands
His limited tools were consisted of
Only those that were made by his hands.

His dwelling was quite humble
It was the interior of a cave
And as such it had no doors
Intruders tend to trespass at their will.

A constant battle to keep his home
And the little things that he possessed
His raiment was made of animals' hide
And so was the covering of his bed.

His rivals were both man and beasts
His god was the flame, he worshipped it
And he kept it burning, day and night
A source of light, heat, and for cooking.

One day, he stumbled upon a tiny tree
Quite attractive, the leaves remind him
Of his hands, five fingers leaves it had
With healthy buds but lacking any fruits.

By then he had perceived a notion
To make a broom with the branches
And so he broke a few of its branches
And placed them in his cave to dry.

He stripped them of the leaves and buds
Then made himself a worthwhile broom
And swept his cabin spic-and-span
Gathering the remnant from the floor
And placed them in a fire to burn.

Soon the seeds and the buds were popping
As the cave was filled with smoke
He felt a daze came upon him
A peaceful one indeed he thought

And with that daze there came a crave
That he consumed a quarter of a lamb
As he beats upon his hollowed log drum
Singing many songs while he dance
Then off to sleep in dreamland he went.

Waves

Wild by nature often they roar
Rolling with boisterous sound
Torn to fragments by the rocks
That they in anger had struck.

Rushing the pebbles and sand
Perhaps a try to settle ashore
Soon their reign does ceased
At the margin along the shore.

Smashing into countless pieces
Of mists that vanish like the air
Or fall back to the watery sand.
To join the salty blue and deep.

Where silent waves roll ashore
With bliss they caress the sand
That spreads its white blanket
To greet those who care to lie.

Or stroll along the tickling sand
As it trickles between the toes
Making itself a friendly gesture
Of an invitation to sit and play.

Whenever they become angry
Their natural tendency which
Is a boisterous roar frequently?
Imposing their fear upon men.

That found themselves terrified
Then begins to revise their plight
If our ships with ease they capsize
What of our little feeble frames?

April

April comes with its showers of rain
And the flowers bloom comes after
The birds all singing their happy tunes.

And children with their jolly laughter
Chasing the squirrels among the shrubs
And frightening the birds to take a flight.

The wild doves in the tall trees above
Peeps down and cooing with suspicions
In the high grass out yonder grazing.

The white-tailed deer and the swift hares
Confined each to their different world
Shaking their tails with popped-up ears.

Keenly listening to keep at bay all threats
Below in the meadow cattle and sheep
Bleating, mooing, and chewing their cuds.

As We Behold

A cultured pearl in Daddy's eyes
A gift, oh, so precious and rare
Nature and love calls it in to being.

A sparkling gem in Mommy's eyes
For the entire world to see it
Perhaps to some, an orchard in splendor.

Sprung from Mommy and Daddy's loins
Now in a cradle smiling with bright eyes
Like an orchard rare freshly bloom.

With little hands and feet like petals
Bright eyes gleaming like little stars
A serene face that calms rage and hate.

A cultured pearl in Daddy's eyes
A precious priceless gem in Mommy's eyes
In the eyes of the world perhaps an orchard rare.

Whose beauty and fragrance attracts them all
Thus a tribute to the world, men, and birds
Bees and butterflies swarm, its nectar to extract.

At First

When first the gleam of light
On that first day we caught a glimpse
Or perhaps it was a night
With a glittering moon and stars
Cuddled gently in Mommy's arms.

When first the sound our ears received
Joy with laughter sighs or cries of relief
Or perhaps it was "Hush, my baby"
Welcome to this your new world
With tender lips kissing your cheek.

Or were we left wondering
What was next to come
When at first a love so dear
With her gentle voice whispering in our ears
Words to which there was no meaning.

But soothing to the ears, saying, "Hush, my dear"
Though we knew not their meaning
When at first we distinguished that voice,
From the many other voices
That enters in our ears.

When at first we tasted the milk
That we pulled from our hosts
Were we cannibals or parasites?
When at first we experienced love
Did we wonder what was next to come?

What was there for us to expect
When at first we came to realized
That one day, we must return
To replenish the earth
From where we originate.

At Midnight

Long after the sun retreat to rest
Midnight and its darkness appear
Inquisitive thoughts now wonder
What sound may enter the ears?

The lack of the children jeering
All traffic seemed to have cease
The robins and the doves are all
Cuddled fast asleep in their nest.

No singing or cooing on the lawn
Absent is the sweet sound of life
When midnight silence appears
In the dark with eerie sleepy eyes.

At Peace

Leave the fight to those who hate
Let them practice their brutal fight
Displaying their rebellious attitude.

Contrary to what he had commanded
They have lacked the inward peace
Thus they choose to roar and fight.

Behaving like the wild savage beast
Leave the stealing to those who are
Consumed with grudge and envy.

One might steal more from them
Perhaps even their precious life
Desperate and faithless scoundrels.

Let them display their envious spirit
Those who steal if they are caught
Will murder to cover up their deceit.

Stealing today will repay tomorrow
By a robber or at the judgment call
Let them live as they may choose.

Hypocrites the heathen and the saint
Judge them not, for the master will
You wish them well, loving them still.

Beauty

Beauty loves you it's easy to see
How it earnestly clings on to you
Never wanting to sever company
Whether taking a swim, or a bath
Washing your face, it never leaves.

Unlike the makeup it never fades
Not even when you are sleeping
Enhanced by your radiant smiles
Love your beauty as it loves you
And while it shows your outside.

Remember there is yet another
The beauty that lives inside you
And when the sin of age begins
Taking hold of its revengeful toll
Upon your fading robe of beauty.

With wrinkled skin and flabby fat
When beauty to the eyes do fade
Let your inward beauty shine out
Like wine it gets better as it aged
Leaving its mark upon the hearts.

Black and White

Once I saw a flower bloom
It sprang from leaves and stem
Wearing only the color green
At first its bud was pale green
But it grew lighter by the day
At last the green was all gone
It adapted to the color white
Until age had taken its course
Again its color began to change
Next it turned into yellow
Then again into brown
In its final stage of beauty
It became completely black
Dried crisp and fell from the stalk
From its bloom until its fall
Its grandeur was its color white
When black and white unite
See their expression on paper
Look now with your own eyes
This white paper dull and bare
Transformed into a story
With these black words
Giving birth to this their new life
Neither could by themselves
Create such awesome wonder
Imagine this being your story
Now, let's speak in regard to fabric
A boring white or a dull black cloth
Interlaced into alluring stripes
If placed in opposite direction
It gives a beautiful plaid design
Black and white as liquid mixed

Produces the color we call gray
And if we should speak of mortals
When black and white multiply
Would that be a white child?
Or would that child be black?
I would rather just a child
Black and white is our eyes
Or would we rather be blind
Or perhaps we would prefer
Choosing the black pupil
Or perhaps the white sclera
One without the other
Or separating them
Would certainly leave us blind.

Blue Caribbean

I placed my foot into the water
Of the blue Caribbean Sea
It was so soothing and enchanting
I could not resist entering in.

Gazing upon the endless blue
That spreads toward the horizon
By then the sun was hanging low
Approaching the ending of the day.

It spread a settled streak of golden line
From my feet straight up to the horizon
With little silvery speckled spots
That seems to be bubbling up and down.

With the motion of the Caribbean Sea
Rocking the world with glee
A wealth of joy my contented soul
Had fostered, from that blissful evening tide.

Thanks to him that lead me here and beyond
For then, I plunged myself into the sea
Soothingly warm as it engulfed me
I stroked in rhythm toward the horizon.

The shadow of the night was drawing nigh
As I then begin to hope
This bliss will never cease
But by then the sun had settled.

Deep below the horizon line
And the moon began basking its gently glow
Like a waltz it glides from beneath
A patch of dense dark cloud.

Presenting itself in a perfect circle
It was a bright full moon at twilight
Basking in the blue Caribbean Sea
The shadows were gone.

And the seagulls had bedded down for the night
But they will return with the sun at dawn
Until then, Queen Moon will reign over the night shadow
Shining in her luster on a glossy Caribbean Sea.

Booth Hill

Booth Hill overlooking a meadow
Frequently you will see the farmers
Harvesting their tall summer grass
Preparing for the winter hay.

Down in the valley all misty at morn
Lies a meadow through which flows
A silvery stream in silence it rolls by
The stream seems to awake at noon.

When it sparkles with bright silver
As the sun keeps beaming down
Then the fawns and the lambs
Drink to quench their thirst.

Then rest under the shady trees
That surrounds the meadow
And line the banks of that silent stream
When at night and all is at rest.

The stream too seems to take a rest
For then at night it loose its silvery sheen
Transforming itself into a golden glow
And sleep under the shadow of the moon.

Many have been carried up Booth Hill
Unfortunately, they were unable to return
There they were given their last farewell
To sleep forever on Booth Hill.

If from their sleep they should be awaken
They would find Booth Hill a pleasant sight
In the winter, it poses a white snow dome
And changes its color as the seasons roll by.

Boredom

Standing alone doing nothing
Has proven to be quite boring,
Idle, and unproductive at best
Some closed their eyes to see—nothing.

That, too, seems to be useless
Hoping they would drift away
In slumber to pass time away
Sleepers are known for doing—nothing

Neither for, or to themselves
Thus naught shall be the gain
Not the reward of one dream
A terrified or a mysterious one—nothing.

The latter should be preferred
But neither would venture nigh
Still continuously wasting time
Sleep now awaken only to gain—nothing.

And bright eyes return to see
What it was that it had missed?
Not a great deal if any was lost
Idly ran the day with the aid of—nothing

A puny price would be the cost
Standing as one the lonely boss
For absent were many thoughts
Sleep was busy killing time for—nothing.

With those precious moments
Sleep had willfully squandered
And those that are left unslept
Are likely to remain awake for—nothing.

Broken Limb

A broken branch was so badly torn
Hanged almost vertical to its trunk
It stood no chance of ever healing
But a convenient ladder it presents
For the climbing visitors venturing
The canopy.

It screeched when the heavy burden
Advanced with trampling intrusion
Thus sweeping the earth beneath
As if being swept by a rush of wind
The nemesis that almost detached it
From its trunk.

The glory that once belonged to this tree
Upon which this branch was attached
In those days of glory hanged a swing
From this broken branch of past fame
Where children often gathered to wait
Their turn.

When they would soar and plummet
To the peak of their childish ecstasy
Propelling themselves with their feet
With hearts thumping beyond belief
No longer would they envy the birds
For flying.

Instead they would mimic the birds
And not only imagine in their minds
Now they stand in pity and in anger
Gazing at a worthless limb dangling
From its trunk with its only purpose
As a ladder.

Broken Spell

For whom the bell will toll
On whom the spell was cast
So many years has pass since then
How long was it supposed to have last.

Now that the spell has been broken
Heaven has opened with compassion
And poured down its love for ransom
Redeeming grace with love fulfilling.

Came in search of a mortal sacrifice
Pure and innocent no need for an altar
Chosen to relinquish this hell call earth
To reign in a higher spiritual plain above.

Leaving a mother's heart badly wounded
That it may never completely heal
With lips that cannot complain in depth
And eyes now dried no tears can fall.

But oh, that silent cry that flows within
Sobbing to the beat of a wounded heart
So numb that no pain can it feel
As the curious mind keeps pondering.

Why did one leave the other behind?
Our dear master did assign to us
Each our different task here on earth
And when our tasks are completed.

We will return to the great beyond
Thus from above we can look down
To guide the others we leave behind.
Towards the path to answer their toll.

Bubbles

A tiny pocket of air is being trapped
Covered by a delicate film of water
A captive prisoner wrapped in a ball.

Too feeble a prisoner this bubble be
At first it doubts its strength to burst
Even from the frailest of prison bars.

Secluded from its own and its home
Often it wears the color of a rainbow
In short seconds their life span cease.

Sometimes kids blow them in the air
Attending a street fair or in the park
Or even locally made in their homes.

Wherever it may be forced to reside
Sometimes they are being formed
From the bed of a pond or a stream.

Trapped below the surface they rise
Struggle upward climbing for the top
Always yearning to burst and be free.

Stifling a description some might say
And if they are lucky to reach the top
They might take their flight to the air.

Now at the end of their short journey
They burst and vanish mixing in the air
A home of freedom where they belong.

Building a Village

A lonely pilgrim or perhaps a nomad
Fatigued of traveling relented to go on
Here where he now stands convinced
To build him a village but first
He must construct himself a home
As the evening shadow begins to fall
Repeating the evenings that has past
Casting a spell to enchant those in view
Never in his travel has he ever seen
Nature with such a magnificence scene.

Not the picture presented in the sky
Nor the portrait of the landscape
Spreading from the green grass at his feet
Traveling up to the never ending horizon line
Or the silvery glittering specs from the sea
Standing in that bay in haw he concluded
Convinced, and committed, that this village
He must make his quest, and begin to build
If not heaven, then nowhere else below
Deserve to be that village he envisioned.

A home in which he must anchor his feet
If indeed life entrusted upon him a pioneer
Then he must obey that which he must.
Then begin to unpack his burden beast
Thus man and beast relax and feed
As he gazed in his mind at the village-to-be
That night he slept and dreamed and visioned
But in the morning when he was awakened
He could not tell that it was a dream
There was no obvious difference to him.

Night or day, asleep or awake, all was bliss
He had found a heaven right there on Earth
In the cool of the morning, he began his quest
Of building a village but first he must
Build him a home to rest his weary bones.
One by one, he hewed down the trees
Labored with his beast to have them in place
Before he was done, his wandering behold
The many neighbors all around him
Staking claims and building homes and a village.

Cease-Fire

Should there be unsettled strife
Between me and thee
I beseech thee to unshackle
Our bond of war
And grant our seeds their liberty
Let it be understood
That there shall be no reckoning
Of death, mine or others
But cease the strife among them
Form a bond of love
Gulping from each other goblets
Sipping a common cup
Feast upon fresh roasted venison
And fine wine
Let them sing and dance and laugh
As neighbor and friends
Bury the feud with me in my grave
If I be buried
Scatter it in the wind or the ocean
If I be cremated
But vanquish our unsettled strife
If there be any
Let them love and be married freely
Banish impeding feud
Let peace and love reigning forever
For now, at last
I will close these weary eyes of mine
With the hope
That our seeds will love perpetually.

May the sun fill you with its energy
By kissing you from head to toe as it rise
Then may the moon smile at you when it departs
And exchange your troubles for a smile

The Night's Farewell

Farewell to this splendid night,
The dawn will greet us soon.
Goodbye for now,
Soon at sunrise you will rest,
And the owls and the bats
Will depart with you.

To return at twilight
To share the night basking
Under the silvery cloud and stars.
At dawn the rooster will
Stroll the lawn picking worms
From the grass covered with dew,

Crowing and boasting
To be the earliest bird,
Enchanting the hens
And awakening everyone.
Soon the nightingale will be singing,
The doves will be cooing.

Then the rest of world will join in.
See the sun slowly peeping
Over the horizon,
Its beaming rays now upstage the moon.
In a little while, it will be noon,
And before you know it
Half of the day will be gone.

Then the night shadows will return
And the sun and the moon
Will exchange their stations.
Farewell to the gleaming rays.
You must relinquish your light
Once again; it is now my turn.

To summon back the darkness once more.
Then the frogs will croak
And the crickets will chirp,
The bats and the owls
Will resume their hunting
While the rest of the inhabitants remain at rest.

My Ancestors' Spirit

There are times when I can sense
The spirit of my ancestors rejoicing
As I beat on my drums with glee
And chanting around the bonfire,
Teaching our men and women of tomorrow
Our vocal history, in ballads of melody.
Despite the literacy that we have been denied,
We teach the young generation our history
In the tradition, just like our ancestors used to do.

Often I hear the voices of my ancestors
As their spirits holler in the wind,
Some moaning, from what used to be
The excessive labor they had encountered
And the lashings from the cat-o'-nine-tails
That they were compelled to endure.
While other spirits were whispering,
With some soft and gentle breeze
Thanking death, to have come and set them free.

Some were bold enough to join the ballad,
Others were shy and hid behind the trees
And I watched them waltz with their kind,
As the spirit of my ancestors had a jubilee,
They seem to have filled the air.
I could sense their presence everywhere.
Infants feeling some strange vibes
From these foreign entities, giggling with glee
From the tickling feeling it brings.

Toddlers beckoning to some entities
Who were hiding behind the trees,
And to those who were brave enough
To join the bonfire spree.
Young men and women unaware
Of their foreign guests, too busy,
Playing Romeo and Juliet.

While the elderly sat and smiled contentedly,
The dogs, too, hound with unusual sound
Sensing the entities that were around.
I heard the spirit of infants screaming
As mothers smashed them against the rocks,
Sparing them that wretched lot
That blackness has cast.

Three Days

Yesterday was a wonderful day;
Everything seems to have gone my way
At twilight, in tranquility I gently whispered,
Asking the sun to stay,
As the sun keeps sinking in the horizon
And its light continues to fade,
I then, with a boisterous shouts of plea,
Still begging the sunlight please stay,
But Mother Nature yields for no one,
Instead, she acts only at her will.

Yesterday has come and gone,
Its short reign of pleasure has surely ceased.
It made its visit and fulfilled its purpose,
Now it is deemed to be the past,
Today has graced us with his presence
Please enjoy it while it lasts,
For those who are overcome by curiosity
Will ask, where have yesterday gone?
And from whence comes today?
Could yesterday reinvent itself into today?

I have tried peeping into tomorrow
But it was nowhere, all was black as night.
I wanted to invite the dawn to make
An early arrival, but I should know by now
That Mother Nature listens to no one,
And she reacts only to her own voice.
If only mortals could see the future,
Then their destiny they could change.
It would be like handing them the key
To open the portal leading to immortality,
Then death would lose its fame.

Each Day

Awaken from my sleep each morning
Anxiously greeting yet another day
Knowing not what challenges it has to offer me
But I accept them anyway
Lacking the luxury of picking and choosing
The task that awaits me this day.

I am well equipped to master them
Because I have the fortitude to endure.
I know not where my challenges lie,
The simple fact is I choose not to care
Though often they take me by surprise.
But I am resilient and willing to adopt,
And I am always eager to try.

With this equipment in my possession,
Sometimes I feel invincible,
Confident to overcome any challenges of the day.
There are times when mountains lie before me
And seem impossible to climb.
That's when resilience steps in to remind me.

There are many ways to the other side.
Over the mountain if I choose,
Around the mountain, or dig a tunnel through.
It will aid me to remember,
That a mountain is only
A valley turned upside down.
I know not why these challenges confront me,
And I simply choose not to query.

It is not for me to wonder why,
Or to sit in despair and cry,
But to be a victor, or to die.
And so, each morning when I rise,
I seldom think of the days gone by but of this day,
Focusing on the task at hand,
How to be a better man.
For today, I will do the very best as any mortal man.

Metaphorical Mountain

The farmers and the shepherds prayed
By our sincere faith
Let this mountain be moved,
With faith as large as the ocean
We pray, make this mountain
Turn into level land
That we may plant our crops
And graze our flocks.

And there upon that mountain stands
Windmills and towers
To generate the village power
And harness the airwaves
For the media broadcasting.
"The mountain is good for us,"
The villagers say.

We pray that it will remain forever,
But neither farmers, shepherds,
Nor oceans of faith
Will remove that mass of land.
Faith can move mountains
Is a metaphor used by man.

Redemption

Crystal gleam from heavenly beams
When the light from that star appeared
With angels from heaven descending,
Heralding the good tidings of a virgin birth.
While shepherds were in their field abiding.

Around their fire they all had gathered.
Angels, and shepherds, praying and singing
Hail to Mary, Joseph, and Jesus, the baby king,
For on this day, to man redemption has come,
And Christ has graced us with his birth.
Upon his head he wears a halo,
An emblem from his birth, honoring a king.
Soon he will wear yet another crown
When upon Calvary's hill he fulfills his destiny
And purges the world from sin with his blood,

A crown of thorns that pierced his flesh
And stained the earth with drops of blood.
Not forgetting the gaping wound
The spear had torn into his side,
All for the redemption of the human race.
Soon angels with him will ascend,
Uniting the trinity once again in heaven.

The house Prisoner

The little old lady, who for several years
Sat on her veranda rocking on her chair,
Viewed with glee the wonders of nature.
As she gazed at the bees gathering pollen,
She saw the caterpillars turn to butterflies.

She enjoyed the music as the birds whistled
Their songs of melody. She even seemed
To be rocking in rhythm with their tunes.
Every now and then, she joins them,
Singing a song, birds and woman intoned.

She would watch the children as they played,
How they waved and shouted their greetings
But all good things must come to an end.
When she abandoned her rocking chair
She had grown weary of the latest fashion.

Young men with trousers below their rump
And girls in garments revealing private images.
She bore the shame and hid behind her drapes
And seldom if ever, did she looked out.
In her house. She kept secluded and cursed
The fashion of what she had seen.

The Hermit

Devoted men and women
Make of themselves slaves
By choosing to embrace
Tedious and unusual quest,
Not for grandeur fortune or fame,
Therefore, for the sake of tranquility
They self-imposed an exile to a lonely life
Confined only to their lonesome self.

Earth mothers or earth fathers
As they are often called,
In search of higher spiritual plane.
To be one with nature,
Withdrawing themselves from their fellowmen
To reside in desolate dark caves,
Or some bewildered forest shack.

No longer hindered by human distraction,
They can now devote their life
To meditation and prayers,
Thereby gaining extraordinary spiritual powers
To perform mysterious feats,
And they are sought-after for healing and advice.

With the use of their third eye,
They are able to maneuver in dark caves
Accurately with ease like the owls and bats.
Hermits, monks, and lama;
They all share a self-imposed exile,
And many leave their footprints called a monastery.

The Frog and the Crocodile

While taking a nature stroll one morning
I stumbled upon a bridge.
Curiosity got the best of me,
And so I started looking over the side
At the chocolate-colored water below.

Frogs were frantically leaping
From the rocks and stumps
Heading toward the banks,
Croaking up a warning, danger is around.
They were strumming up a chorus,
A rather annoying song.

I stared in wonder at the water below,
And the ripples were still expanding.
I gazed with inquisitive thoughts
Of what the show might be,
But nothing except the ripples moved.

Well concealed in the center of the ripples
Were two eyes staring back at me.
A crocodile had visited for his morning meal.

Compass Plan

On the road to nowhere
Simply because you had failed to plan
While others who start behind you
Now they are up ahead
And looking back at you
Misguided and confused, baffled with no plan.
A plan is a chart and a compass,
A necessary tool for our success.
It guides us from the very beginning
And all the way to the end.

Traveling in circles,
Absent of any landmark, failure to have a plan,
it appears as if you are blindfolded
Or traveling in the dark
Walking over landmines and trespassing
Where there are foes.
It would've been wise to have made a plan
To pilot you on your way.
How would you know where you are heading
If you have no clue.

Adopt the principles of the master craftsmen.
They all have a plan.
So does the successful businessman
And everyone else but you.
Vanquish your game of chance
And make yourself a solid plan.
You will find life less challenging
And a clearer path to tread.
A plan is a compass that guides you
Along life's rugged pathway.

The Phoenix

The Phoenix, as the Greek legend goes,
Rose from its ashes and took flight,
Soaring up to the sky above the clouds
Where no one has ever gone before,
Reinventing itself, and became revered.

    It exemplifies courage and self-will,
    A lesson the Phoenix taught the world.
    Feats that appear to be impossible
    Can come through
    By executing the principle
    Conceive believe and achieve.

The Phoenix refuses to fret and idle
Or to accept defeat in any way,
But instead with determination,
Hard work and perspiration
It build itself a heavenly home.

    Where other creatures
    Were scared to venture.
    But he was unselfish, and never satisfied
    Even though his house was a fortress.
    It was concerned about the rest of the world,
    Especially those who unfortunately
    Went astray, and were caught up
    In a blizzard of substance abuse.

The Phoenix embarked on a quest
With the principles conceive believe and achieve,
And once again, the Phoenix,
Led by example
And set unbeatable standards.

Building houses for those who went astray
And were caught in a blizzard of substance abuse,
Pioneering the way, making it possible
For others to rise from their depression,
Take flight and reclaim their lost status
With the creed, conceive, believe.
And they, too, will achieve.

A ruler that rules with an iron fist
Seldom wins, if ever
For though he may have won many battles,
His men would have soon lost their zeal.

This Moment

Yesterday is gone forever
With the assurance
It will never return,
And while there may
Never be a tomorrow;
At least not for some.

Then let us cherish
Each moment today
With sincere gratitude;
Let us now dismiss ourselves
Of our evil thoughts,
If only for today, while we
Constantly remind ourselves
That we are in this race to win.

And winning, as we know it
In its most simplistic form,
Is just to see yet another day.
Yesterday is behind us,
Now today we are simply
Striving for tomorrow.

With one goal to keep in mind:
To be a better person comes tomorrow,
If only to accomplish one good deed
By aiding my fellowman if in need,
And when my day confronts me
And there remains no more tomorrows
I would hope my last words will be
Peace on earth, and goodwill to man.

The Nightingales

pair of nightingales as punctual as the sun
They greet each dawn with their singing
And farewell to the sunset, singing in duet
They seem to have their favorite tune
Or perhaps it was the only one they knew.

> But certainly they had their favorite tree
> Because there were many on the lawn
> They even had their favorite branches
> The highest branch toward the east at dawn
> And the lowest branch to the west at twilight.

At sunrise, they gaze toward the east and sing
And with glee I watch them serenade the sun
At dusk they perched upon the lower branch
And stared toward the west singing lullabies
Until dawn, when they return with their songs.

> As punctual as the sun singing joy to the world
> Or perhaps they were thanking Grandma
> For the bits of bread she used to toss them
> With precise timing at the first line of their song
> Grandma was always there to greet them,
> With a piece of bread in her hand.

Houses of Dreams

Our nurseries are the cradles
From which we build
Our houses of dreams.
Where our seeds are sown
And our thoughts and ideas blossom.
These houses of dreams
Are where we cultivate the dynamic leaders
Of our future, our youths.

Houses where dreams grow into reality,
Bearing the first fruit on the moon.
Houses where fragile minds,
With coaching, grow up to be
Intellectual giants.
Such as our founding fathers were,
Who attended great houses of dreams
To build us a strong foundation.

Our houses of dreams,
Which our architects from granite built
Upon firm foundation
On which our glorious nation stands.
With education being the corner stone,
Of every modern successful society.
Why then are our craftsmen, the teachers,
Being cheated with such a measly wage.

They who mold
And nurture the brilliant minds,
The giants and leaders of tomorrow
Our glorious nation,
Scientists, lawyers, doctors, and politicians—
They all are made possible
By the underpaid, casualties of our society,
The nurses of our cradles, our *teachers*.

Crippled

Pierce through the blackness of the night,
Shone two beams of frightening lights.
Two terrifying eyes stood perplexed,
Crippled by the startling beam of lights.

And a strange, confusing rumbling sound
Accompanied that dazzling light
Along with an annoying foreign smell
That tickled the nostril as it intruded.

A smell slightly like the heated one
That came in the forest and took our grass
With the color of the leaves in autumn
Just before they fall or the flashing streak
Before the thunderclaps with little spots,

Like fireflies bursting in the air.
And when it left, all was as black as this night.
And now I must find me a new place
To rest for the night and graze on the soft grass
That's moistened by the dew, in the morning light.

Over yonder beyond this track of unknown beasts
With their crude shapes and black round feet,
Some with a lonely jockey, others with many,
Two legs, four legs, even eighteen and more,

Some my size with two antlers
Which the jockey grips for his rein,
Others several leaps from hind to nose,
But none of them with a tail.

How do these unknown beasts move so fast?
And what funny sounds they make.
The driver looked at the startled, transfixed deer,
Came to a screeching halt and blew his horn.

The deer was still puzzled and transfixed.
Then at last, the driver put out his headlights
And watched the deer canter off to the other side.

Cry

Cry little boy, cry
Even if you know not why
Because soon, very soon,

Even of that too
You will be deprived.
For when you disrobe.

The cloaking of your youth
And accept the status of manhood,
Then the world will tell you.

That a man is not supposed to cry
Without supporting facts
And void of rational reasoning.

So cry little boy, cry while you can
Even if you know not why.
Laugh little boy, laugh.
Because soon, and very soon,
Your laughter will be limited
When the cares of this world.

Fall heavily upon your shoulders
With too many burdens to bear.
So laugh, or cry, little boy.
Laugh or cry while you can.
Let all your emotions run wild
While you are still a child.
Because soon, and very soon,
They all will be subdued.

Intrusion

An incident intruded upon my eyes.
It was quite disrupting.
It came suddenly, without warning,
Too abrupt impossible to ever be denied.
It was so disturbing,
A softer heart would have cried,
And so it pierces through
Only to touch the inward me.
There it trespassed and settled,
Then claimed its throne as king.

I often hear its boisterous shouts,
Evict me if you can.
When at last, I fall asleep,
And thought the battle I had won,
But again it came to me in a nightmare,
As vivid as when I was awake.
Intrusive sight, embedded in my core,
I hear its annoying roar.

When eyes have seen and mind conceived
A constant reminder, evict me if you dare.
Intruded upon my eyes,
Now trespassing on my brain,
But with time, it will slowly disintegrate.
For in the past, time has shown
That the heart will heal its wounds
And this, too, will heal with the passing of time.

Paradise

That perfect place.
A classic piece of real estate,
A paradise, one that is perfectly
Governed by my own standard.
For I have found my paradise,
It lodges deep inside of me
Beyond the realm where
Feeble mortals are forbidden.
Out of reach, out of sight,
Even beyond their imagination.

Not some prime real estate,
Or like that garden of Eden,
But incapable of human intrusion.
I have found my paradise
To be a tranquil state of mind.
As king of my paradise,
I reign supreme, myself and me alone.

Where I can be at rest, and be at peace
With the world and me.
Buddhist priests, hermits, and monks
Are all on a quest for paradise.
I guess they all know of it,
Because they all choose some solitude.

Seduction by a Queen

Pour upon me warm water
Water from a Nubian stream
Not as frigid as frozen water
Or hot as lava expelled from a volcano
Just as warm and soothing
As our body temperature
Springing from the fountain
Of Africa's queen.
Water comes rushing like the Africa's
Great Victoria waterfall
White water comes foaming
With sweet delight.
Queens singing and princes alert
With their spears erect.
When all is calm,
The water settles down below,
As the rushing water
From those fountains spill.
Mist, forming rainbows,
That often two heart's desire.
Douse me with water,
To chill this heat upon me,
Pour it on my head,
Let it trickle down to my feet.
Let me dive into the river
That rushes to your sea
Saltwater, of Africa's Queen,
Come rushing over me.

When upon an African Queen
I lay my longing eyes,
I sat in the snow to rid the heat
That came upon me,
Nubian queens, of many shades,
Ebony, chocolate, almond vanilla
And chestnut brown,
With charcoal-black curly hair
And well-endowed from head to toe.
It seems the Creator
May have favored you more,
Pour upon me your warm water.

*Peace is not the result of fighting;
But to the contrary, it is the product of
Avoiding those that could have been fought
But never was.*

Retrospect

In existence today, stands a product
Of yesteryear's bygone confusion,
Not just a figment of my overactive imagination
But indeed a reality,
Retrospectively surveying the illusions
And confusions of my youthful heart.

    In retrospect, I glance at my yesteryears,
    When I was blinded with confusion.
    I now view the past
    With the eyes and wisdom of today
    And identify my faults.
    I had perceived many illusions,
    Stemming from the desire of my youthful heart,
    Often unable to distinguish some illusions
    From realities that transpired then.

In my illusions, I have seen
Vivid pictures painted on blank canvases,
Mirrors that do not reflect,
Their pictures are all trapped inside,
Like old mirrors that have faded with time,
Too bleak, too far back in time
To reflect or to reminisce
On those distant yonder years left behind.

    Now in my later years, retrospectively
    I reminisce on when life was innocent
    And the world was bliss.
    For now, with thankful lips and my prayers sincere,
    I am grateful, dear Lord,
    For your guidance along the way.

Open Doors

The door is open.
Will you please tell me,
Why are you still here?
It seems that I have grown
Far too much accustomed to this life.
I know no other way, and if I did
Probably I would be too scared to try.

See that hamster treading on that wheel,
Could it be that I am similar to it?
Just too simple to realize
It can stop the treading
Whenever time it wishes.

Look above your head.
See those captive lovebirds
SHanging in their open cage?
Did you say captive birds
With wings that can fly?
And yet they remain in an open cage.

Yes, they made themselves captive.
They know no other place,
And they refuse to try.
The door is open, and I refuse to leave.
Why am I still standing here, why can't I try?
Like those emancipated from slavery
And remained on those wretched farms.

They say that men are creatures of habit
And we are afraid of the unknown.
The master kept them illiterate
To have them under his control.
I am afraid I hold myself captive by fear,
Dare not to exit through the open door.

But if I don't, then I would be no better
Than that simple hamster,
Those silly lovebirds,
Or the dependent slaves.
My fears I must leave behind me,
And walk through that open door.

Overcast

On the double, batten down the hatches
And secure all the gears.
There is a fearsome storm fast approaching,
And its wrath we must reap.
Unlike any storm you have seen,
This is not just a simple gale
But with hell-bent havoc.

Look at the clouds!
See how they are all dark and gloomy.
They are telling us beware.
Lightning flashing, and thunder clapping,
The waves are roaring and growling fiercely.
They double their sizes in minutes
They seem to be extremely angry.
In all my years at sea,
This is the weirdest overcast
My eyes have seen.

Pull up the anchor fast,
And loosen the mooring lines,
Cast off for the deep.
Release the captive ship
From the harbor wall restrain,
And let her freely sail.
Ships were made for sailing the waters
And not for anchoring in a port.

For soon we will lose both ship and harbor,
Colliding against the tide.
Erect two mooring ropes, from the stern to the bow,
One on the starboard and the other on the port.

If one must venture above on deck,
Be sure to use them for your lifeline.
Sound the alarm, all hands off deck.
We will weather the weather down below,
Facing it head-on, in the eye if we must.

Striving

Never condemn yourself for the things
That others have done.
Neither condone with their wrongs.
And if they are indeed your friends,
Then think it over very carefully
About the friends that you keep.

Choose your words very carefully,
Because they should be your bond,
And as such you should live by them.
Honor your commitment when you can,
And strive to avoid deceitful act and strife.
Doing good is always a noble act.

But you must strive for the best.
It's more acceptable in life's race,
And often will boost your morals
To heights beyond petty thinking.
Grudge no one for what they have gained,
For you too can achieve the same
If you apply with the proper aim.

The best is that status
That hangs on a silvery cloud.
And when you have done your best,
You have earned yourself a golden crown.
But this I beg of you to remember;
That great heights were never attained
By more sleeping, and less toiling or thinking.

Fire Men

Fighting men of great valor
Dressed in black with yellow stripes
With knee-high boots
And unusual-looking hats.

With yellow luminous
Stripes on their clothes.
Huge red trucks with ladders
And hoses, off to their death-defying feats.

With pride they rise to the occasion
For fighting fires, the fire brigade.
Each time they bravely respond to a call
They were on their way to hell.

And each successful visit they made
Extinguished the devilish flames.
I hope they know they made the devil mad
When they put out his flame.
Gallant men of bravery bred,
They who risked their lives while aiding others,
Search and rescue the pits of hell,
Ventured smoke-filled, oven-hot rooms.

Searching closets, where frightened children
In panic may be hiding in dark, damp, restricted space
That often reminds them of a coffin.
Oh how sad when we lose them.

Whether on or off their field of battle,
Thus, while they are alive let us
With honor thank them,
Our gallant men, our fire brigade.

First Kill

The tip of the front sight post
Was halfway up,
And centered from left to right
In the rear sight aperture
That defines bull's-eye,
And so he slowly squeezed the trigger.

Then a single bang rang out,
Followed by a flash of light
Expelled from the nozzle of his weapon,
With the smell of gunpowder
Now potent in the air.
As the bullet sought for its victim.

It found its spot and made its claim
And laid its victim to rest in peace.
The target was no more in sight,
He was overcome with a different feeling.
This was not a practice on the range,
But what was once a living soul
Was sent to greet his Lord and Maker,
Never again to roam.

He held his breath
For what seems to be eternity.
But in reality
It was only about fifteen seconds.
Temporarily paralyzed,
He stood like a statue.
Then he made a huge sigh,
As he muttered, to do or to die.

That was his first kill,
And so he tried to convince himself
That he might have missed,
Thinking that his arms
Were not as strong as they should have,
Or perhaps the wind was blowing
A bit too strong
And affected the windage,
Or he might have jerked the trigger and missed.

Half-Open

A door was left half-open.
It was hanging by just one hinge,
Presenting a crooked display.
It was leaning at an angle,
Hindering the full flow of the sunlight.

From the window across the room,
You could see it formed a beam of light
That showed a perfect seven in the morning light.
And as the morning passed toward the noon
The seven grew progressively smaller.

Then exactly at noon, it disappeared
Only to reappear on the other side of the room.
But now it reversed the picture,
And the whole room now filled with light
Except for a little dark shadow it now cast.

As the noon passed toward the evening,
That little dark shadow began to grow.
And so it grew into the twilight.
Then soon darkness consumed the room,
For the night had fallen upon us.

Halves

Two halves, that could not be one
Too alike, that they cannot be distinguished
Or sometimes, they are extremely opposite,
Too different for them to peacefully coexist.
Regardless of their differences, we call them twins.

Some of them are physically attached,
So complex they cannot be detached.
And those we call conjoined, or Siamese twins
But still, they cannot be considered as one.
Oh so close, and yet so far from being one.

Each has the ability to think on their own,
Having dreams and fantasies of their own.
Two halves that cannot be made in one.
Two left feet, quite an impossibility
And two right shoes a clumsy stride does make.

Still, twins remain as separate entities.
Some two halves can never be made as one.
But there are also those two halves
That are compatible in every way
And exist in harmony. As one they fuse,
Making null the word confusion.
Two halves can indeed become one.

In the Shadow

Standing in the shadow
Not particularly wanting to be seen
Or to be recognized,
Not really hiding
Simply just low profiling
To lower the tempo down.
Occasionally when the light gleams in my direction
A silhouette it sometimes revealed.
Standing in the shadow
Taking the time out to absorb the game,
From the prospective
Of being on the outside looking in.
Stop being a player, if only for a while,
And sit among the audience
And become a spectator,
Watching the game of life
Being played on the world's stage.

Standing in the shadow
Blending with the night,
There I can see clearly, but not easily be seen.
And in the shadow, I developed a nocturnal vision,
Thus observing the evil deeds
That transpire within
And learn to identify my oppositions
And cast no light for them to see.
Standing in the shadow
There I often see
Reality overshadowed by fictions,
Deceptions, and cleverly manufactured illusions.
With all the world a stage
And each individual a performing actor
Or a captive audience, held at bay.

The world today is in disarray,
Concealing its evil in conspiracy,
Cloaked under the shadows such as the government,
Its laws, and the darkness of night
Standing in the shadow
Growing weary of its gloom
I reclaimed my former position
Playing in the game.
Not exactly highlighting or high profiling,
Just an average player
Performing on the world stage.

Infinite Now

Infinite now,
Tell me how can this be?
When with each tick of the clock
A new now has passed.
Centuries gone by, that were once now,
With each fraction of a second
Rolling back with time.

Thus, that which was once now
Is forever confined to the past,
Lingering for millions of years
While as in the now we speak.
And the words we utter
When departed from our lips instantly
They become the past.

While each single fleeting moment subsides,
There to dwell eternally in the past
Infinite now, or eternal past,
Tell me what is time?
If not just an inadequate tool
To measure the seconds and the years we pass.
Infinite now, how can this be?

When soon days ahead we call the future
Will mimic the now and they too will be vanquished,
Dissipating in the void past
When their reigning of time is ended.
Then like the sands of time
That trickle through an hourglass
As the future becomes the now.

*Love stay awake with patience,
Gently, calm, at rest, alert and ready
To assume the position when eventually
Hate does lose its faith.*

Innocence Lost

Because infants personify innocence,
They know no guile, they display
No hate, no fear, no malice, or deceit.
They possess no crafty or foul intention.

Doubtlessly this is such a cruel world.
They will soon find out
When their innocence
From them gradually is stolen.

First when introducing them to pain
By slapping on their cheeks,
Unable to fathom why.
In their confusion, they learn how to cry.

In the midst of their confusion,
They also learn to pinch, scratch,
Poke others in the eyes
And bite others youthful hides.

No foul or envious words they know,
But soon they will learn them.
But for now they only mutter cries
Pleading for their comfort.

Soon this cruel world will teach them
Grievous and vulgar words,
Grievous words that stir up anger,
After which violence will pursue.

Jack Frost

It's now Jack Frost's time to rule
The Sun has given up his reigning
And have gone a vast distance away,
Too far for its heat to penetrate heavily
On this side of our planet, but just enough
For us to see his golden circle and its silver rays.

So Jack Frost came with his frigid self
And painted the north all in white
He usually comes around once every year
To serve his quota, a three-month period.
Mr. Frost was predictable, one could say.

But for the past several years
He has been fooling us
And made some random visits.
Now it is impossible to predict his coming
With any form of accurate pattern.

He even went out of his boundary
And entered in the south.
He got the farmers all worried
When he ruined their crops,
But that was not exactly Mr. Frost's intention.
Instead it is called global warming.

Just Before Sunset

This evening, the sun and the moon
Synchronized in their coexistence
As the Sun was heading west to rest.
It has traveled vast, across the globe,
But now only a short distance remained
Before it reached the horizon to rest.

There it will depart until the morrow
While the semicircular moon,
Still holding its own, faintly gleaming
With just enough glow to show its presence
Above them both, stood a silvery dome,
The sky above, made both their homes.

The sun now casting its shadow short
And soon its reigning will end
For the twilight shadow has drawn nigh
To see, the sun and the moon, both aglow
With only the absence of the stars
To complete the celestial trio.

Know Myself

Will I ever completely know myself? And if or when I do,
Then what have I learned about myself?
Those are among the pondering questions
That come to me.

And with those questions, an answer came.
For now, I have found myself to be a child,
And I beg of the world, please teach me
Because I have also come to realize.

That as a child I know not.
My desire is to move forward,
And to take with me, if not the world,
Then as many as I can.

And in my hour of darkness,
I will meditate on the light,
And by faith it will appear,
Thus changing that which I can.

For there is more to our lives
Than us, feeble mortals, dare to fathom,
For Elohim, Adonai, Yahweh,
Jehovah God hath made it so.

Mango Season

As the dawning of the morning appears
And the birds in search of their first meal
Perching upon the mangoes to feed,
Loosening them from their delicate stem
And they plummet to the ground.

Oh how often they must have wished
If only they have hands to hold them.
As the mangoes fall from the trees
Swarms of flies and insects
Surrounding them to feed.

While the strong acidic odor
Of the rotten ones
Smells like a pub the morning after
Celebrating a victory party
For a World Cup soccer game.

Some well concealed
Among the clustered dry leaves
That form a bed to cushion the fall,
Some landing, still unblemished,
As children search among the leaves to feast.

Then the animals rummage
Through the remnant for what is left,
The pigs sniffing around, then plunging
Their snouts and uprooting the leaves
For the hidden ones they have found.

My Pride

After just one fall,
Too stubborn to surrender
After hundreds of falls,
My pride keeps telling me
You haven't tried them all.
Rise up and stand tall
Life must end before you quit.

If with doubtful hearts we pray,
And lacking faith and pride in ourselves,
Then our dreams we too frequently slay.
But when with faith and pride,
Endlessly we strive to achieve,
Often our strength increases,
Giving credit to our pride.

There are some things
One should not compromise,
For if they do, doubt and fear
Will claim the inward man
And vague becomes their pride.
Then they surrender and die.
Your pride is your courage
And the principles for which you stand.

Be too proud to accept less
Than what you are worth.
Be too proud to settle
For a second-class man.
Be too proud to stay down
While blood still flow through your veins.

Ransom

Which is it? Is it time, or is it destiny?
Which of these powers have me
Under their control, like their puppet?
They pull my string, and I do their bidding.

Some power has demanded my later years
As a ransom for my silent pen. In my earlier years,
I have kept my pen a captive,
Concealed from the eyes and ears of the public.

Which power is it that acts as my judge,
My juror, and my executioner?
For I have been found guilty and sentenced
For my remaining years as a slave to my pen.

What then shall I say but thanks?
To whatever the power that intervened
And fused me with this, so great a love, my pen,
For within this world no greater joy could I find.

Snow White

Grandma made her visit to the library
And there she took her a seat
At the center of the stage.
She trapped my eyes,
And I was delighted to see
An aged rose vine,
Still blooming in her splendor.

Her crown was like a mountain peak,
All covered with snow.
She was beaming,
As if the sun was wrapped around her.
She sat erect, and displayed well
Her snow-white locks
That glitter like a golden crown,
Grandma a queen upon her throne.

Though not as brisk as a maiden's stride,
She moves gracefully
And kept her head up high.
She sat and read, without the aid of spectacles.
For hours I watched her yesterday
While her snow-white locks
Were still gleaming as radiant as the sun.
Yesterday I saw my literature Olympian
With her snow-white hair.

And if not viewed by others
Who were graced with her presence
As a literature Olympian, a Queen,
Or a goddess of the sun,
Certainly she was quite an inspiration,
Because she brightened up my day.
I am glad to have met Snow White
At the Eastchester public library yesterday.

Sweet Chariot

Riding on the backs of others
As parasites to achieve
With a firm belief
That the end will justify the means
With no concern for others,
Just selfish and greedy.

Willing to sell their family
And friends just to achieve.
Being a parasite, they
Sing sweet chariot, let me ride
On the backs of others.
Sweet chariot, why let them ride,
Never thinking of others?

No such thing as having pride
If riding chariots of injustice is allowed.
Sure they will ride,
Fact or fiction,
Finding ways to justify their greed as need
When they hear the cries
From the children whose parents
They have cheated.

They try to justify themselves by saying
If only your parents had worked
A little harder and longer.
Why was this curse placed upon us?
It may help if one explains
How our transgressions differ
From any other nation?

Why linger this yoke
Around our neck for so many centuries?
And if this is not a curse,
Then tell us where did we go wrong?
Or should I believe
That we are created unequally in his image?

The Forest Dweller

An old man lived in a forest with his son
His cabin they built on the riverbank
The boy he knew no other home
For there from a lad he and his father lived.

They built the cabin with their hands
The only playmates that he had
Was the animals that came around
Though at first they were timid and shy.

But as time went by their fears subsided
And soon they began to play with him
His father had long since gone to rest
Some forty years since then has passed.

Now the forest becomes his domain
He calls the animals by name
And often shares his cabin with some
He became their physician and bound their wounds.

And mended their broken bones
He spent most of his time
Watching the ducks floating by
And fishing minerals from the river.
He used the jewels gathered from the river
To cover his cabin floor
Following the tradition of his father
Diamond garnet gold and other precious stones.

That twinkled like stars on his cabin floor
His wealth was immense as others found out
But to him they meant nothing more
Than a gleaming or a glittering floor.

The Little Flame

A little flame, though not visible to everyone's eyes,
Lingers inside to keep a constant glow, and burns
As the source of our energy, while we remain alive.
Not bright enough to attract intrusive wandering loiterers.

But bold enough to deter the evils that lurk in the dark,
Reminding the darkness there is no room for two.
For if this little flame does refuse to glow and surrender
To the dark, what then would we have
left but a darkened, cold heart?

A little flame that radiates within our very core, and
Keeps our hearts warm; that little yellow flaming luster,
Expelling our energy to infuse with that of the celestial,
Giving birth to a halo, deflecting the evils that surround us.

The little flame that guards and warm the nucleus
Of our being, now wraps itself around us
To keep us all secure. Now it has grown and spread
From the heart to a halo that now surrounds us,

Thus attracting likewise spirits to create a positive vibe,
An infusion we call love. Perhaps the dearest of our emotions,
But certainly, the most delicate of them all. And so that
Flame with its invisible glow, acts not only as our guide,
But our protector, and Cupid as well.

*Love and hate are both the same
However, in their confusing state
They are unable to decide which
Will be good or bad that moment.*

The Little Voice

My soul, the governor of my life,
That little voice that dwells within
Acting as my conscience and constant guide.
Always gentle and mild
When sadly furious passion
On its rampage running wild.
And even then my soul
The governor of my life,
That little voice remains serene and calm.

My soul. What becomes of it
When I lay down to rest?
Does it wander off traveling around
On some odyssey and reveals itself
In what I call a dream?
Or does it stick around standing guard
Watching over me while I sleep?
The little voice that always whispers
And directs my path, and frequently
It reminds me that it will never
Leave me alone.

My soul, that little voice.
There are times when I hear two,
And I am unable to distinguish
Which is my governor,
And act contrary to my little voice.
Then things never work out right.
And even then, my little voice
Never treats me rash,
Even when I falter.
My soul, that little voice,
The governor of my life.

The Clown

I laugh, because it seems to me
That I am unable to cry.
Of that emotion I have been denied.
Regardless of how fiercely I may have tried,
The well for my tears are all dried.

Be thou not mistaken,
There are many sorrows in my heart.
But of the tears, nay, I dare not shed.
What force is there that shackles my tears?
Why will my tears not flow?

And so, I dedicate my life
In being a clown, and laugh
Because I am unable to cry
While making myself a laughingstock,
Placing smiles on others faces,
And painting a mask on mine.

Should one day, those shackles break,
And the wells of my eyes replenish
From its drought,
Would I then cease from laughing?
Nay, I don't dare to cease from my laughter
For a clown is deemed a doctor of glee.

Thus, for a dampened spirit,
I prescribed a dose of laughter
At least once per day,
But as many as your heart desires,
Without the risk of an overdose.

Seven Days

If traveled vast to yonder and back
A journey in time, that seems to have no end.
Time past, or future, back to face our Sunday
Where, on our first week, God begin his creation
For seven days, that man deemed to be weak
With no apparent difference to distinguish them
One from the other, no color shape or size
Or even variances in their hours, all twenty-four.

Sunday, when most reserve for their soul
To worship and greet each other in spirit.
Soon the night visits us and Monday appears,
Then back to our laborious task, but soon
Monday will turn its back, and Tuesday
Will creep right in with no visible difference,
Only the date to which they are assigned,
And the once stocked refrigerator starts to diminish.

Wednesday, the midway optimist or pessimist,
It took a neutral stand, Thursday will decide.
Today is Thursday, how can you tell?
No change in color, it sounds and looks the same
Excepting for the refrigerator, which is now almost empty.
The juice bottles are low and so is the milk jar.
Tomorrow will be Friday, with some notable differences
The seafood for lunch and supper, and a measly check.

Show Your Love

Did you let someone know that you love them today?
If so how did you express your love?
If they were words, were they genuinely from your heart,
Or mere wind that easily and quickly dissipate in oblivion,
Or words too faint to be audible,
Or perhaps so vague that they soon be forgotten
Without evoking a thought or stimulating a feeling?

Did you shake a hand and smile today?
Or maybe a pat on the shoulder or a hug?
Did you let someone know that you love them today?
Did the deaf old man hear you say you love him
When you greeted him with a warmhearted smile?
I guess he did, because he returned
A much bigger and brighter smile.

Did you let someone know that you love them today?
Did the blind boy at the corner hear you say you love him
When you grabbed him by the collar and pulled him back
Before he heard the screeching brakes
Of the car that ran the stoplight?
I guess he did, because he said,
"Thank you, my friend."

The mute tells you that they love you
When you see them nod their heads,
With radiant smiles and sparkling eyes
Twinkling like little stars that complement their hearts
And revealing its contents.
Love demands more deeds than words,
And our deeds reveal the intents of our souls.

Show all the love you can, as often and as long as you can,
To as many people that you can,
Remember, love works no ill.
Be sensitive and tolerant to our human imperfections.

Sir Gallant

Finally, their paths had crossed.
He had searched and found his king,
And now upon a new quest he must begin.
He raised his sword, then pointed toward the sky and held it
As he stood erect upon his ivory-colored stallion
While glancing upward, then he gently bowed his head
And placed his clenched sword firmly to his chest.

That was their honorable salute among those warriors
Showing and sharing their mutual respect.
He then proclaimed, "Greetings, I herald thee, my lord,
My sword and my life to this land, I bid,
With thee as my commander and king."
And thus a bond they had created,
And his pledge of allegiance he had given.
Side by side over hills, valleys, and plains they roamed.

Often death they deprive, living by their swords,
Performing feats that seem like miracles,
Without fear or concern that a day of reckoning will come.
Blood flowing like a crimson stream,
Warriors and beast drenched from head to feet,
Your ivory-colored stallion now covered in oxblood red.
You have never shunned a fight,
And now upon this perilous eve you lay.

With sword clenched in hand
And shield firmly gripped with iron will.
That fatal blow now taking its toll,
Your strength is fast depleting; in minutes, it will be gone.
Not one single drop of tear, or any sign of fear.
Farewell, my comrade, fare thee well,
Your sword has served this land well.

Side by side, many tedious battles we have fought.
Sir Gallant should be your name.
While steel was clashing and sparks were flying,
You have never lost your nerve, neither faltered or despaired,
Constantly advancing never retreating or losing a foot of ground.
Up gleamed a gently smile across his tranquil face
Proclaiming victory and relief.

He knew his day of reckoning has come,
And pleaded, "Please, prop me up against a sturdy oak tree,
One that fits a gallant warrior such as me,
For today, my maker, I shall meet."
While what was once his ivory-colored stallion
And faithful companion,
Now covered in oxblood red, franticly cantering in circles
And stopping just where he laid,
An obvious invitation for him to remount.

But something strange has happened,
And it was clear to both man and beast,
Though overcome with agony, he managed to repeat,
"Please prop me up against a sturdy oak tree so that I
May fall on my sword and end this agony."
"Now before you depart, my faithful subject and friend,
As your king, I bid thee farewell my comrade, fare thee well
I dub thee, Sir Gallant, forever be your name."

Sleep

Sleep, that remarkable resemblance of death,
That tranquil haven, where the body and soul
Retreat to rest in their fortress of dreamland.
When, with the closing eyes, reality aborts itself,
And life transforms into its heaven or its hell.

Sleep, that time when your imagination awakes
From its dormant sleep, and fantasy comes to life.
When your fears confront you to a fight or flight.
Then at last you are awakened, drenched in sweat,
From the challenges of your sleep, fearful plight.

Sleep, that borderline between alive and dead,
Where many have visited and are unable to return.
And if you make a conscious choice not to visit him,
He will sneak up on you and kidnap you anyway.
Sleep, the mystery that mimics death, and possibly
The gateway to the afterlife.

The Street Corner

On our street corners,
Where sweet doo-wop melodies once reigned
With harmonica and accordion.
In melody they charmed our streets,
Placing a pleasant smile of glee
On our beloved commuter's faces.

Now, if not a frown,
A false smile is being worn as a mask
As we watch the fading glory of our streets
And those now standing at the corners.
If only we could turn the hands of time
To where doo-wop once reigned.

Mobile drugstores on bikes,
Or loitering sitting on some parked car,
A bulge in their waist that marks their pistol;
And two on either side
One bulge marks the cash and the other
Indicating the drugs for sale.

Whispering while you pass,
Still advertising their products on the low.
Red bags, pink bags, yellow bags,
Green bags, blue bags, and purple bags;
Scooters, wheelchairs, walkers,
And crutches, all maimed from the game.

The night ladies, provocatively dress
In their flimsy seductive attire;
Fiends advertising their products for sale,
A thirsting habit to quench.
Some, victims of economic failure,
And the others simply are exploited.

The Statue

A sculpture stood high upon its mound
Anchored well and permanently fixed,
Its profile looking down over his shoulder.
He seems to be watching everyone who passes by.

He stood in a gaze with his mouth half open
As if he was asking, "Haven't I seen you before?"
There seems to be several of them.
They all are dressed in different clothing.

At nights, he is illuminated by the street light,
And in the days the sun casts his shadow
As it moves respectively from east to west.
This sculpture seems to appear everywhere.

The sculptor who carved that statue
Had made a duplicate of himself,
And often people who pass by would wonder
Have I seen this somewhere else before?

*When problems appear unsolvable
Like an impossible mountain to climb
Remember that a mountain is nothing but
A valley turned upside down.*

The Stallion

Oh, how I regret losing the days
When at my free will I roamed the prairies
Galloping, cantering, walking,
Or even standing still.
Those were always my choice.

I traveled as a highly ranked
Member of my herd,
And never had a weary mile.
Where I felt to linger I did,
Grazing on the fresh grass.

In the watery meadows, all at my leisure.
What fun I had wandering the plains,
Prancing, trotting, and galloping,
Playing with the mares and fillies.
Oh, how short-lived my joy.

When man came and restricted me
And then they stole my liberty,
Like they did the Indians and the Blacks.
Now frequently I am whipped into submission;
Yes, I was deprived of my free spirit.

They labeled me domesticated
And placed a harness on my head
To lead me where they will.
Constantly upon my back they sit,
Like kings upon a throne.

When not forcing me to race,
They dress me up for their circus
To laugh and have their fun.
Standing on my hind legs
Is awkward, and it hurts.

The Shepherd's Light

A perilous night on a stormy sea
No moon or stars were there to see.
The sky was black as the shepherd's coal
That which he used to fuel his fire.
A ship adrift with the crew in despair
When lightening rips the dark night air
Revealing a dim speck of light.

They piled inside their lifeboat
And headed towards the glow.
Soon they found a shepherd's cottage without a door.
Good shepherd can we enter in
The shepherd replied, it is for that reason
Why I hang no door
I am a shepherd for men, my flocks are my company.

Over the years, numerous souls I have saved,
And I have shed likewise as many tears
For those that I could not aid.
See that grove over yonder,
As far as your eyes can see
I have planted a tree for each corpse
That washed upon this shore.

And from those trees, I have burned the coal
To fuel this flame that rescued you.
Then let us build a lighthouse,
One that towers towards the sky
And shines its beams for miles around
That we can be its keeper, and a shepherd too.

The Rose

Their beauty are rare,
Their fragrance soothing and enticing.
Thus, in and out between the petals
A paradise, where birds and insects rest and nest.

The busiest plot of ground in the garden
Where they skillfully exhibit their favorites,
And sometimes unique maneuvers such as the butterfly.
How they poise motionless on a rose or a flower.

Or the hummingbirds, how they hover still,
One barely detects the movements of their wings
With their long, needlelike beaks
Penetrating the flowers and feasting with delight.

Upon those splendid roses they perch with pride,
Mildly jostling for their turn at the grandstand.
Soon, one by one, the petals from those stalks will fall
As day by day, their beauty slowly fades.

And when all the pollen and nectar are depleted
And their beauty now is lost, only a slender stalk
standing lifeless and bare, long cease the frequent visits
From the birds and the insects.

But every now and then, a lonely dragonfly
Stops and rest its wings. The flowers and the roses
have lost their beauty, and their fragrance dissipates,
The garden no longer the favorite attraction.

Nature had run its course,
And soon the lifeless skeletons will no longer stand.
Then the birds and the insects will move on
To another upcoming beautiful attractive plot of ground.
And so the cycle of life continues, on and on.

The Red Oak Tree

A lad, who from his birth
Had been deprived of his sight
To him all was as black as night.
And though he had experienced
Much by his given senses,
An old red oak he had yet to touch.

And so he traveled along
This road each day from birth,
Through rain, sleet, snow
And the scorching sun,
And found himself a shelter
Along his way home.

One hundred and fifty paces
From the railroad track
Heading north, toward the mountain;
That's where the shelter begins.
For it was there, that he noticed.

The rain was no longer
Beating on his head.
But he could still hear the sound
Of the raindrops beating faintly
As if they were being suppressed.

He also heard the crisp leaves
As he touched them with his cane,
And the sound of the crumbling leaves
Beneath his feet.
He heard and felt, but could not see.

And he knew not from whence
That shelter came.
And in the blistering sun
For a hundred paces was a shade
With breeze, like that of a giant fan.

And so he pondered upon
The source of his shelter
While searching with his cane.
Where and what can this be
With no structure of bricks or stones?

Searching while he roamed,
Swiping his white cane from left to right;
Then at last
Upon this massive structure
He encountered.

And feeling his way, he walked around
This massive object,
Fifteen paces in a circle to be exact.
He tried to put his arms around it
But he needed many more
To span that massive, old red oak tree.

About the Author

Ventilating with his pen has ranked pens among Norman Smith's best friends simply because he loves to write and would not have it any other way. He is an honorably discharged veteran of the United States Marines, with one of his first poems entitled "USMC Brothers," at which point he still hasn't kept a record of his writing. Since then, Norma wrote another poem entitled "Mother" which he gave to his mother for a Mother's Day gift. She framed it and kept it on her wall until she passed away. It was then Norman's niece came across the poem and asked him to read it at the eulogy. It was well accepted by family and friends, from whom came many compliments and encouragement to expand on his writings. He took their suggestions and began to compile a collection of poems, so here he is, sharing his thoughts with you.

Printed by Libri Plureos GmbH in Hamburg, Germany